With this book, you ar
many will reject but Hi

—Cristina Cain
Prophetic Minister
Author of *You Can Hear God*

From the opening pages, I knew I was reading a rare and priceless new scholarly treatment of eschatology.

The author explores critical areas of End Times with sound Biblical exegesis and perceptive spiritual insight. Lou Comunale unapologetically debunks and accurately interprets and clarifies key misunderstood concepts such as The Great Tribulation, The Day of the Lord, The Wrath of God, the Timing of the Rapture, and God's End Times Providence for His Children. Having studied dozens of mainstream and popular theologians on End Times Prophecy over the past 45 years, I can say with surprise, excitement and joy that this book turned my preconceived Pre-Tribulation Rapture view on its head. With great love and care, this theologian imparts timely and indispensable clarity and understanding. I now know how it unfolds and what I need to be and do to ensure the Lord's protective hand of grace through the upcoming time of increasing calamitous trouble on earth.

Fear and confusion have been replaced by peace and honest expectations of what lies ahead for those who trust and love their eternal Lord and Savior. I truly hope and pray that multitudes upon multitudes read this book!

—Kris V. Long,
Kindle Reader

If you sense we are in the end times and the second coming of Jesus is near, this book is by far the most comprehensive and easy to understand description of the Great Tribulation and Day of the Lord. Lou has a supernatural understanding of the scriptures and makes an undeniable case against most common accepted theories adopted by the church for many years. He proves common beliefs are not based on scriptures or facts at all. Such a good read by a very gifted author! (on my way through reading it a second time).

—**Mark DeVelde**
Amazon Reader

I'm only about halfway done, but I'm already truly blessed by the book. Started last night, couldn't put it down all night. I am coming from being a Pre-Tribber for most of life but never was 100% able to trust in it. Now I see why! THANK you brother. Many want to live in this deception, I prefer to walk in the Lord's truth and find comfort in knowing I am prepared for what is coming.

—**Christopher Maskey**
Amazon Reader

Lou Comunale simply lays out and examines all the end times Bible scriptures with a profound clarity, in a unique communicative writing style, that is captivating, intriguing, easy to read and easy to understand. After over 40 years as a Christian, reading numerous books and hearing innumerable messages on the hope of the pre-trib rapture, I was always left more confused with all the twisting and distortion of charts, time tables and diverse interpretations. Reading this book felt like a friend took me by the hand, walked me through the scriptures, connected all the dots and now am finally able to see and understand the simple end times truths clearly revealed in the Bible.

—**JoBeth Kested**
PIT Crew Ministries

ESCAPE
THE COMING
ANTICHRIST

ESCAPE
THE COMING
ANTICHRIST

**WHEN THE PRE-TRIBULATION
RAPTURE FAILS (AND IT WILL!)**

LOU COMUNALE

DEDICATION

To the readers of this volume who love and embrace the truth of God's word and who understand that the current events taking place in the news today all lead to the long-awaited return of Jesus Christ. To those who are not afraid to accept the truth of the Pre-Wrath rapture, though it may go against the popular teachings of the day, may this volume bless you with tools to defend the truth.

CONTENTS

ACKNOWLEDGMENTS

I thank my Almighty Father God, who from my earliest years gave me an insatiable hunger for the truth and an earnest expectation for the return of our Savior Jesus Christ.

I thank the Lord who gave me grace and insight through the Holy Spirit in understanding the parallels among Daniel, the Olivet Prophecy and Revelation in a way that powerfully reveals God's timeline for Christ's return.

I thank my church pastors who impressed upon me to always "prove all things" on the topic of eschatology (the study of end-time events), and to not accept any doctrine that conflicts with any portion of scripture.

I thank certain teachers of the Pre-Wrath doctrine who have produced material which I've referred to, in part, in compiling this work. Among them are Robert Van Kampen, Charles Cooper, and Chris White (not to mention the early church fathers, all of whom believed in the Pre-Wrath position).

I want to thank those who helped me with this project, especially my intercessor JoBeth Kested, my proofreaders Colleen McCallister and Christina J. Donato, and my ministry friend John Ramirez.

Thank you, all!

FOREWORD

I thank God for Lou Comunale. I met Lou four years ago through another ministry. He is a man of character, a Godly man, and he has a special anointing on his life through the Lord Jesus Christ to reveal, to share, and to teach the truth of God's Word to the Church at large about the end times.

In his new book, **Escape The Coming Antichrist,** he reveals a lot of spiritual insight to bless the Church today, so the Church will not only be ready, but be equipped for the times that we are living in, and in the times to come.

John Ramirez
International Evangelist
John Ramirez Ministries

INTRODUCTION

Can Jesus return at anytime?

Can He return *tonight* to secretly snatch up His saints *before* He actually returns in glory at His Second Coming? Most evangelical leaders will thunder in the affirmative. But most only use half of the scriptures available on the topic to come to that conclusion. In essence, some scriptures have been *Left Behind!*

Knowing only half of available information can only lead to trouble and error. There's a funny moment in an old comedy movie where someone is leaning against a bathroom wall in front of a sign reading, "MEN." Another man walks through the door and is soundly booted out by a woman inside. The first man walks away from the partially obscured sign and we now see that it actually reads, "WOMEN."

It's just as important to have *all* the available information to understand any doctrine in scripture. God's Word says, *The SUM of your word is truth!* (Ps 119:160, Revised Standard Version), *sum* meaning *all*.

One needs to connect *all* the scriptures together in order to fully understand any topic outlined in the Bible. And when you find a pattern where scripture does not conflict with one another, *then* you'll have the full, true picture.

To suggest that Jesus can come at ANY moment in time – *tonight*, in fact! — many teachers cite various scriptures to try to prove that point:

- *Behold, I come as a thief* (Rev 16:15)
- *For yourselves know perfectly that the day of the Lord so cometh as a thief in the night* (1 Thess 5:2)
- *I will come on thee as a thief, and thou shalt not know what hour I will come upon thee* (Rev 3:3)

Well that sounds quite convincing, until we include the *sum* of God's words and then we get a better, and *different*, understanding.

Notice what Paul says here: *But ye, brethren, are not in darkness, that that day should overtake you as a thief* (1 Thess 5:4). On the one hand the Word says that Jesus will come as a thief, then it says – to His faithful followers – that His return will not surprise *them* as a thief would.

Can we see the pattern? Can we discern what He's saying?

The *only* people who will see Christ's return as a *thief in the night* are going to be those who do not believe in, nor prepare themselves for, His return.

Let's break down and explain what Paul says in the above verse.

> *But of the times and the seasons, brethren, ye have no need that I write unto you.* [That's because they are already knowledgeable about the 'times and seasons' for His return!] *For yourselves know perfectly that the day of the Lord so cometh as a thief in the night.* [The Day of the Lord is the actual return of Christ, and it's going to come as a 'thief in the night,' but to whom?] *For when they shall say, Peace and safety;* [Who says 'peace and safety'? Why this is when the Antichrist system shall have so overtaken the world that there's

no one to fight against them!] *then sudden destruction cometh upon them,* [By Christ's judgments upon His return!] *as travail upon a woman with child; and they shall not escape.* **But ye, brethren, are not in darkness, that that day should overtake you as a thief.** [See the comparison? Christ's return will come as a 'thief' to those in the world, but not to His true followers, who understand the 'times and seasons.'] *Ye are all the children of light, and the children of the day: we are not of the night, nor of darkness. Therefore let us not sleep, as do others; but let us watch and be sober. For they that sleep sleep in the night; and they that be drunken are drunken in the night. But let us, who are of the day, be sober, putting on the breastplate of faith and love; and for an helmet, the hope of salvation* (1 Thess 5:1-8).

Jesus explains here what it means to *be watchful*:

Watch therefore: for ye know not what hour your Lord doth come. But know this, that **if the goodman of the house had known in what watch the thief would come, he would have watched, and would not have suffered his house to be broken up.** [a *watch* was a designation of time within the night hours; similar, in a way, to the phrase, *times and seasons.*] *Therefore be ye also ready: for in such an hour as ye think not the Son of man cometh* (Mt 24:42-44).

Luke's account makes it plain that those who are watching for His return are not going to be surprised because their whole heart is in doing the work of the Lord, i.e., *occupying till He returns* (Lk 19:13):

But and if that servant say in his heart, My lord delayeth his coming; and shall begin to beat the menservants and maidens, and to eat and drink, and to be drunken; The lord of that servant will come in a day when he looketh not for him, and at an hour when he is not aware, and will cut him in sunder, and will appoint him his portion with the unbelievers (Lk 12:45-46).

Conversely, Jesus chides the Sardis church for not watching:

Be watchful, and strengthen the things which remain, that are ready to die: for I have not found thy works perfect before God. Remember therefore how thou hast received and heard, and hold fast, and repent. ***If therefore thou shalt not watch, I will come on thee as a thief, and thou shalt not know what hour I will come upon thee*** (Rev 3:2-3).

So, all in all, the *thief in the night* analogy refers to one's non-readiness rather than to Christ's imminency. And imminency is a chief, albeit unbiblical, "proof" for the pre-trib teaching. As much as we'd love Him to, Jesus can't come tonight.

But we've been taught otherwise.

You're going to find while reading this book that we have been misled about a wide range of topics and issues surrounding eschatology. Some of the positions taken in this book may not make the author popular, but expounding the truth is a far more desirable goal.

So, yes, there *are* "watches in the night" and "times and seasons" which indicate the timing for the Lord's return. It can't happen beforehand. It will occur during a fixed, pre-ordained chronology of end-time events that *must* take place *before* His return. Do you know what to look for so that you're not caught off guard by the contradictions of various teachings?

Interestingly enough, the *thief in the night* analogy harks back to a phrase that Jesus uttered about working while it's day because *the nighttime comes and no man can work"* (Jn 9:4). Jesus is telling us that the thief will come upon the church in the *nighttime* when the church is no longer able to operate openly. It is during this *time and season* that the church – being in the Great Tribulation -- should expect the Lord's return.

While reading this book, you will find that many of the supposedly *best* pre-tribulation scriptures are all twisted beyond their biblical intent. And many other scriptures have been conveniently *Left Behind* (ironically) in order to arrive at a pre-trib theory.

I like to engage with people on Facebook regarding their pre-tribulation beliefs. Invariably, they will defend the position that says Christians will not be here during the Great Tribulation. They insist that they are already raptured before the seven seals of Revelation are unsealed.

And how do they arrive at that conclusion? They will defiantly point to their Holy Grail of pre-tribulation scriptures, Revelation 4:1.

Enjoying the opportunity to teach, I reach for a bible and casually ask, "Okay, can we go to that scripture and see what it says?"

> *After this I looked, and, behold, a door was opened in heaven: and the first voice which I heard was as it were of a trumpet talking with me; which said,* **Come up hither***, and I will shew thee things which must be hereafter. And immediately I was in the spirit: and, behold, a throne was set in heaven, and one sat on the throne...* (Rev 4:1-2).

After reading this go-to scripture for the pre-trib rapture, what is *your* opinion of the verse? Can you truthfully defend the pre-trib position that this is, indeed, a pre-trib church rapture? There's actually no reference to the church and there's no reference to a pre-trib rapture. But they insist that the phrase, *come up hither,* refers to the rapture. So I calmly ask, "But who was told to *come up hither*, the Church or the Apostle John?"

Almost like a prosecuting attorney, I prod the witness, "And why was he told to *come up hither?* Isn't it true that John was told to come up to heaven in order to receive revelation knowledge so that he could go back to earth and write the rest of the book of Revelation?"

"Your Honor," I usually conclude, "I rest my case."

You would think that might settle it, but sometimes *no!* They may double down and insist that the Church is raptured because the Church is not mentioned again after Revelation 4.

Well, how can there be no church on the earth and, yet, scripture tells us that "saints" will still be on the earth? At what point did church and saints become mutually exclusive? Is it possible that *the night has come when no man can work* means that the church has to go underground during that time of persecution? That's why, henceforth, you only hear of them referred to as saints.

Surely, they wouldn't have concluded that the church has been whisked off the earth if they'd only read the previous verses in the book of Revelation, where they would have seen that the Apostle John affirmed that the last four of the seven churches are *on the earth* at the time of the Great Tribulation. You may not believe that, but continue reading and we'll explain that in due time.

Unfortunately, I've never seen anyone fess up and say, "You know what? I'm mistaken. There is no church rapture in Revelation 4:1."

Sadly, truth, common sense, logic and reason do nothing to dissuade our predetermined position. Sometimes, we just want to believe what we want to believe and we won't be diverted. We just need to be careful that we allow the truth of scripture to shape our doctrine and not the other way around.

The confusion rages through all parts of eschatology. For instance, it's all too common these days for alarmists to point to various national leaders on the world's scene and declare them the Antichrist. Recently it seems that every U.S. President that comes along is labeled the Antichrist. Will you know the Antichrist when he comes? Will he come from New York, Rome, Ankara or Mecca?

Some will be so deceived that they won't even be able to accurately pinpoint the true *Christ,* as they will erroneously point to *this* Christ and to *that* Christ (Mk 13:21).

Such times of confusion! No wonder the Lord warned His followers to *not be deceived!*

Meanwhile, many have, understandably, been seeking solace in a pre-tribulation rapture, hoping that this will keep them protected from the Great Tribulation and the sure persecution that is coming upon the saints. But they misunderstand the *watches in the night* and the *times and seasons* that pinpoint the timing of the rapture. They also have so exalted the pre-trib rapture to such heights, that they have begun calling *that* the *blessed hope.*

That's not the *blessed hope* my friends. *Jesus* is our blessed hope. *While we wait for the blessed hope—the appearing of the glory of our great God and Savior, Jesus Christ* (Tit 2:13, New International Version). The rapture is not our ticket to Jesus. Jesus is our ticket to Jesus. Remember that there were many saints who have lived and died over the centuries who have never experienced the rapture, yet are right now in the presence of their blessed hope, Jesus.

I want to reassure all of you that not everything about the end times is negative. First off, Jesus will never leave us. And, secondly, we will find that God will provide daily supernatural, miraculous protection for His elect, as He did when He led ancient Israel into the Promised Land. When we carefully examine the scriptures, the Lord does indeed provide a way of escape for His people during the Great Tribulation that does *not* involve the rapture!

This sounds preposterous because all we've known is the pre-tribulation rapture and we've believed that we won't be here during the Great Tribulation. Our focus and energies have been in allaying our fears and dulling our understanding into a false belief that we'll be gone before Antichrist appears. And so these hopeful scriptures – and *hopeful they are* – which we will examine in this book, should buoy our hope as we embrace the biblical *way of escape* and relinquish the stronghold of a pre-trib rapture, which is not going to happen (as we shall prove).

What is needed these days is a simple, straightforward biblical teaching on the return of Christ, the timing of the rapture, and the protection of the saints so that we're *not tossed to and fro with every wind of doctrine* (Eph 4:14).

We will also explore some of the other eschatological scriptures that were *Left Behind* in order to give a more comprehensive and revealing overview of Christ's return.

The teaching in this book should be the new paradigm for the Church to understand the Last Days, since it was the original paradigm recorded in scripture. Hopefully the Church as a whole will embrace this truth. Many seem to be content with only listening to teachers telling them what they want to hear (2 Tim 4:3). Nevertheless, the *Remnant* – which I sense you are – will embrace this truth.

Each of the following chapters have been carefully and methodically laid out so that the reader can come away, step by step, with a clearer understanding of end-time events than they've ever known before. Get ready for surprises and revelations as we examine the great truths of God's word to prepare a people ready for Him, that *we may be accounted worthy to escape all these things that shall come to pass, and to stand before the Son of man* (Lk 21:36).

1
ANTICHRIST PERSECUTES THE SAINTS

As the Doomsday Clock nears midnight, there is nothing more important than to understand the Judeo-Christian scriptures relating to the end times. Our modern culture, tarnished by an anti-God curriculum in the nation's schools and universities, has been dismissive of the Bible. Yet the Bible is the oldest religious book on record. And it purports to explain the conditions that will prevail on the earth at the return of its Savior, Jesus Christ.

So, whether agnostic, atheist or believer, it's imperative to examine the scripture as it relates to the days we're living in now.

Yet with so much confusion and differing opinions from Christian leaders, we must ask ourselves, "Did God intentionally write the Bible to be misunderstood?" Or, are we somehow not connecting the dots properly?

Many believe that the Church will be swept away in a rapture *before* Antichrist's appearance. But, clearly, there are scriptures that say Antichrist persecutes the saints. Which viewpoint is correct? Are they *both* correct?

In the chapters to come, we're going to lay down some firm biblical landmarks in the end-time scenario – landmarks that cannot be moved, twisted or corrupted. Once we identify these landmarks, we will have a firm grasp on the timeline of end-time events. In this introductory chapter, let's first settle the question of whether or not the Church is on the earth when Antichrist appears. And, while doing so, let's also explain some of the more glaring misunderstood scriptures.

Let's begin by looking at a startling pronouncement made by Jesus in the famous Olivet Prophecy. He says that there will definitely be a time of worldwide chaos that marks the end times.

For then there will be great tribulation, such as has not been since the beginning of the world until this time, no, nor ever shall be. And unless those days were shortened, no flesh would be saved; but for the elect's sake those days will be shortened (Mt 24:21-22, New King James Version).

Now this one scripture is pulsating with so much information. First off, there *is* a Great Tribulation period to come. And it is just ahead of us now. It will be the worst period of time the world has ever known. It will be a time so fierce, so frightful, that it has the capability to wipe out all life from the earth! Sound far-fetched? Not anymore!

Not only does scripture say that, but current events declare that this is an *inevitable* course for mankind.

In order to dismiss this prophecy for today, some argue that this scripture was fulfilled in the destruction of Jerusalem in 70 AD. That can't be. Christ says that this Great Tribulation would be unequaled in the world's history. (The New International Version renders this as *unequaled from the beginning of the world until now – and never to be equaled again.*) There can't be two times of great tribulation worse than any other.

We find that there were more millions of casualties in World War I than in 70 AD. So, 70 AD could not have fulfilled this prophecy – end of story! (Yet 70 AD was indeed a type and forerunner of what is to come.)

World War I couldn't have been the Great Tribulation either, since the casualty count in World War II dwarfed the casualty count in the First World War. Only *now* can the stage be set for the worst time the world has ever known. Only in this hour of our present generation can the nations of the world, using nuclear warfare, literally destroy all life from off the face of the earth.

But I want you to notice another important element in that prophecy. Those days are *cut short!* And, why are they cut short? Because if God didn't cut them short, there would be no flesh saved alive on the earth. That's what it says! But – now get this! – *for the elect's sake* – the saints of God who are still living on the earth — *those days will be shortened* so that the world and the last remnant of humanity will not be totally obliterated.

If the saints are in heaven already at this point, this scripture makes no sense at all. Let that sink in.

It is the elect of God *still living on the earth* – not having been *raptured!* – that causes God to intervene to *end the tribulation.* That's the same elect that Jesus Christ comes to rescue, upon His return, *after* the Great Tribulation (Mt 24:29-30):

> *Immediately after the tribulation of those days ... He will send His angels with a great sound of a trumpet, and they will gather together **His elect** from the four winds, from one end of heaven to the other* (Mt 24:29, 31, NKJV).

THE ELECT – JEWS OR CHRISTIANS?

It's interesting to see that pre-tribulationists tend to deny every scripture that shows that Christians are still on the earth at the time of the Great Tribulation. They invariably find a way to say, "Oh, that's not what it's talking about." So, true to form, pre-tribulationists flat-out reject the claim that the *elect* are even Christians, and insist that the elect are God's physical, chosen people *Israel.*

But scriptures say otherwise. In the above verse, for instance, when Christ comes to gather His elect after the tribulation, is He rapturing up His Church or the Jews? That should settle the case right there. But pre-tribulationists would rather have us believe that Jesus is resurrecting a physical people, than to embrace a post-tribulation rapture.

Here are other scriptures to prove the *elect* are, indeed, Christians:

> *And shall not God avenge **his own elect**, which cry day and night unto him, though he bear long with them?* (Lk 18:7)

> *Put on therefore, as the **elect of God**, holy and beloved, bowels of mercies, kindness, humbleness of mind, meekness, longsuffering* (Col 3:12)

> *Paul, a servant of God, and an apostle of Jesus Christ, according to the faith of **God's elect**, and the acknowledging of the truth which is after godliness* (Tit 1:1)

> Peter writes his epistle to the **Elect** *according to the foreknowledge of God the Father, through sanctification of the Spirit, unto obedience and sprinkling of the blood of Jesus Christ: Grace unto you, and peace, be multiplied* (1 Pet 1:2).

Can the previous scriptures, especially the last one, be talking about anyone else but Christians? Of course not! But if we needed more proof, the checkmate scripture of all is this next one. Here Paul distinguishes between physical Israel and God's born-again children, leaving us no doubt that the *election of grace* (Rom 11:5) is God's Church.

> *What then? Israel hath not obtained that which he seeketh for; but the **election** hath obtained it, and the rest were blinded* (Rom 11:7).

"GONE BEFORE ANTICHRIST COMES?"

You've often heard pre-tribulationists say that the Church won't be on the earth at the time of Antichrist's persecution of saints. (Oh, the irony of that last statement is so telling and so contradictory!)

To force scriptures to say what they don't, pre-tribulationists have to insist that the Bible is talking about two groups of Christians. The first group is the Church (which is raptured up *before* the Great Tribulation) and the second group is the scattered saints that come to Christ *after* the rapture.

So, let's examine this point. Paul has a great many things to say about this. Let's begin first by showing that when Christ returns, the *dead in Christ shall be raised up, then we* [Christians] *which are alive and remain shall be caught up together with them in the clouds, to meet the Lord in the air* (1 Thess 4:15-17).

Notice that, upon Christ's return, the raising up of the living and dead saints occurs simultaneously; the dead in Christ rise first, then the living saints follow instantaneously (1 Cor 15:50-54). It is an organic whole that cannot be divided. Christ is reclaiming His *entire* Body, His *whole* Bride!

It is here that Jesus claims the wheat for His barn (Mt 13:30), transforming both the saints who are alive and those who died in Christ into immortal, spiritual beings (1 Cor

ESCAPE THE COMING ANTICHRIST

15:50-54). There is no more room left for any *saints* to be remaining on earth at that time. Just as in the days of Noah, once the door was shut, there was no more opportunity for others to board the ark. In both cases, God removes His own followers after which swift judgment is sent upon the earth's inhabitants. **It is a major fallacy to believe that Christians are remaining on the earth** *after* **the rapture!** Are we willing to believe Christ's own words that no true Christian or Saint is left behind on earth after the rapture?

> *And this is the Father's will which hath sent me, that of **all which he hath given me I should lose nothing, but should raise it up again at the last day** (Jn 6:39).*

There is no room in scripture to prove that there will be a second rapture to accommodate the second group of saints. Nor is it suggested that there are two resurrections of the dead saints. Christ promises that He will raise up *all* of His own upon His return at the Last Day, or the Day of the Lord.

> *And this is the will of him that sent me, that **every one** which seeth the Son, and believeth on him, may have everlasting life: and **I will raise him up at the last day** (Jn 6:40)*

> *No man can come to me, except the Father which hath sent me draw him: and **I will raise him up at the last day** (Jn 6:44)*

> *Whoso eateth my flesh, and drinketh my blood, hath eternal life; and **I will raise him up at the last day** (Jn 6:54).*

Once the resurrection of the Church occurs, there are no more saints left on the earth – *period.* **As we will see in**

14

this volume, as soon as the rapture occurs, swift judgment comes on the earth.

Let's now go through a chapter in Second Thessalonians where the Apostle Paul affirms that the Church will *still* be on the earth at the time Antichrist arises.

> *Now we beseech you, brethren, by the coming of our Lord Jesus Christ, and by our gathering together unto him* (2 Thess 2:1).

Notice, Paul reassures us that the return of Jesus *coincides* with *our gathering together unto him* – the rapture.

> *That ye be not soon shaken in mind, or be troubled, neither by spirit, nor by word, nor by letter as from us, as that the day of Christ is at hand* (2 Thess 2:2).

Paul affirms that even back then there were ministers spreading great confusion over eschatology, specifically, the timing of end-time events. *The day of Christ* that Paul refers to is another way of saying *the Day of the Lord.* Keep that phrase in mind as we continue this volume. So much confusion surrounds eschatology because people cannot accurately identify the Day of the Lord.

> *Let no man deceive you by any means: for **that day shall not come, except there come a falling away first, and that man of sin be revealed,** the son of perdition; Who opposeth and exalteth himself above all that is called God, or that is worshipped; so that he as God sitteth in the temple of God, shewing himself that he is God* (2 Thess 2:3-4).

Paul explains that the Day of the Lord (Christ's return) cannot come *until* two things happen first. This should give all teachers pause when they say that Jesus can come *tonight!*

He can't. They need to read what Paul is saying here. Two things must happen first: 1) a falling away from the Church occurs; and 2) Antichrist arises and takes his seat as god in a new Temple that shall be built in Jerusalem. As we continue we will see how point number two actually *begins* the Great Tribulation.

It is not a coincidence to see that the falling away occurs just as the threatening Antichrist is gaining power against the people of God – *that is why the falling away occurs.* Christians that are on the fence spiritually with God will be more inclined to deny their faith and submit to Antichrist, rather than accept persecution and/or martyrdom.

Furthermore, is it possible – and we're addressing those who believe they will be scooted away in a pre-tribulation rapture *before* Antichrist arises to persecute them – is it possible that they can lose heart and compromise their faith because they were taught that they wouldn't be here when Antichrist arrives? Their unbiblical expectations will have been shattered by the harrowing reality occurring during the Great Tribulation.

This is a major theological point that must be considered. *If* one believes that the rapture takes place *after* the Great Tribulation, one is better able to prepare for it and seek God for safety and protection during it. However if one believes that they won't be here for the Great Tribulation – and suddenly *they are* – they are in worse shape! They may be met with a crisis of belief that they were not prepared for and for which they may not recover: hence, a falling away.

This *falling away of the saints* won't be comprised only of those who believe in the pre-tribulation rapture, but they most assuredly are a part of that number.

There will be people offended by this last point and will not accept it. But that's exactly what Jesus warned us about in the parable of the sower. Speaking of the seed that doesn't get much of a root system:

> *...for **when tribulation or persecution ariseth** because of the word, by and by **he is offended*** (Mt 13:21).

Notice that they get *offended at tribulation*. No wonder *this* message will offend many believing Christians. We present this truth so that people don't fall away when the time comes. Many now can't even believe that God would ever let them go through any type of persecution. Many now don't even have the faith to endure the slightest bit of tribulation for the Lord. But Jesus was always forthright about the Christian life. He told us bluntly that it was a "narrow way" that few would embrace and that we should expect "persecution." Why did He tell us that?

> *These things have I spoken unto you, **that ye should not be offended*** (Jn 16:1).

If we accept these truths now, we won't be offended later. As Luke tells us:

> *...and that **we must through much tribulation enter into the kingdom of God*** (Acts 14:22).

Therefore it's imperative for us to rise up, buck up and be strong. Review the scriptures pertaining to the end times. We will find that the Lord has indeed given us *hope* in end-time scriptures. We've unfortunately only put our hope in the rapture. So take a fresh look at the end-times scenario and really *prove all things* in the scriptures. Let's not be easily misled into believing that our security is in a rapture. It's not. It's in our Lord and Savior Jesus Christ.

THE ONE WHO RESTRAINS

Pre-tribulationists try to use the next scripture to prove that Christians and Antichrist do not meet together at all. After

Paul describes the Antichrist as one *"who exalts himself and defies everything that people call god and every object of worship,"* (2 Thess 2:4, New Living Translation) he says this:

> *Don't you remember that I told you about all this when I was with you? And you know what is holding him* [the Antichrist] *back, for he* [the Antichrist] *can be revealed only when his time comes. For this lawlessness* [Antichrist spirit] *is already at work secretly, and it will remain secret until the **one who is holding it back steps out of the way**. Then the man of lawlessness will be revealed, but the Lord Jesus will slay him with the breath of his mouth and destroy him by the splendor of his coming* (2 Thess 2:5-8, NLT).

Many try to say that the *one who is holding back* Antichrist's appearance is the Church. That way they can make the argument that the Church *steps out of the way* (is raptured) before the revealing of the Antichrist. Now how can we biblically prove that the Church is holding back the appearance of the Antichrist?

Let's think this through logically. Some might argue it is because of the Church's very presence on the earth – that the Church *repels* Antichrist. Well, the Church is certainly not holding back the *spirit of Antichrist* today, is it? We see the Antichrist spirit all over this Nation and the world (1 Jn 2:18, 4:3). So how could the Church hold back the Antichrist?

Besides, scripture shows us that the Church has to go underground at the time of Antichrist! Jesus refers to it as *the time when no man can work* (Jn 9:4). Once the Antichrist forces arise against the Church, the scriptures make scant mention of the Church any longer. And, from then on in scripture, you only hear of the persecuted saints.

> *And he* [the Antichrist] *shall speak great words against the most High, and **shall wear out the saints***

of the most High, and think to change times and laws: and they [the saints] *shall be given into his hand until a time and times and the dividing of time* (Dan 7:25)

And there was given unto him [the Antichrist] *a mouth speaking great things and blasphemies; and power was given unto him to continue forty and two months. And he opened his mouth in blasphemy against God, to blaspheme his name, and his tabernacle, and them that dwell in heaven. And it was given unto him to make war with the saints, and to overcome them: and power was given him over all kindreds, and tongues, and nations* (Rev 13:5-7).

Therefore the one who restrains *cannot* be the Church or church members for the Antichrist is persecuting God's people. Thus, if we have eyes to see, this is another one of pre-tribulationists' sacred cows burnt to a crisp.

Some also argue that the one who restrains is the Holy Spirit. Well, if the Holy Spirit leaves the earth, how in the world can we still have persecuted saints at the time of the Great Tribulation? It is self-evident that if there are saints on the earth, the Holy Spirit has to be here as well.

The only biblically plausible conclusion we can make as to the identity of the "one" who restrains is Michael the Archangel. Let's review a couple of related scriptures.

*And at that time shall Michael stand up, the great prince which standeth for the children of thy people; and there shall be a **time of trouble** such as never was since there was a nation even to that same time: and at that time thy people shall be delivered, every one that shall be found written in the book of life* (Dan 12:1).

Notice that when Michael the Archangel, who protects and defends God's people, stands (as in *taking a stand* to do something), then suddenly there is a *time of trouble* on the earth – such as never was before.

That phrase sounds just like the time that Jesus referred to, which we quoted earlier in the beginning of the chapter.

> *For then there will be great tribulation, such as has not been since the beginning of the world until this time, no, nor ever shall be. And unless those days were shortened, no flesh would be saved; but for the elect's sake those days will be shortened* (Mt 24:21-22, NKJV).

Therefore Daniel's *time of trouble* is Matthew's *Great Tribulation*, because there can't be two "*times of trouble/tribulation*" that have no equal.

Daniel 12:1 gives scant details about what Michael exactly does when *taking a stand* in heaven. Then let's follow the preferred method of understanding doctrine in scripture. It's found in Isaiah 28:10: *For precept must be upon precept, precept upon precept; line upon line, line upon line; here a little, and there a little:*

So let's locate in scripture any other clues about when Michael *takes a stand,* preceding the Great Tribulation. And we find it here:

> *And there was war in heaven: Michael and his angels fought against the dragon; and the dragon fought and his angels, And prevailed not; neither was their place found any more in heaven. And the great dragon was cast out, that old serpent, called the Devil, and Satan, which deceiveth the whole world: he was cast out into the earth, and his angels were cast out with him...Therefore rejoice, ye heavens, and ye that dwell in them. Woe to the inhabiters of the earth and of the sea! for the devil is come down unto*

you, having great wrath, because he knoweth that he hath but a short time (Rev 12:7-9, 12).

This is the true *Star Wars* battle of all time. Michael and his angels take a stand by casting Satan and his fallen angels out of heaven. They are humiliatingly hurled down to the earth with a thud. Satan will have no more access into heaven to accuse the brethren (Rev 12:10). Satan's attempt to usurp the throne of God Almighty has been dashed and settled forever. The demons then take their rebellious anger out on those who are alive on the earth.

Once Michael ejects Satan from heaven, Satan unleashes his wrath upon the Church through the one he's been grooming, his *son of perdition*, the Antichrist!

> *And they* [the people of the earth] *worshipped the dragon* [Satan] *which gave power unto the beast* [Antichrist] *...**And it was given unto him** [**Antichrist**] **to make war with the saints, and to overcome them** (Rev 13:4, 7).

We will find as we continue in this book that some saints will give glory to God by giving up their lives in martyrdom and other saints will give glory to God by being protected from Antichrist until Christ's return. But for now, as an aside, let us explain the use of the biblical phrase *"time, times and half a time,"* to which we referred earlier, and which shows the timeframe for the persecution in the Great Tribulation.

DEFINING TIMES

There are three scriptures that use the phrase *time, times and a half of time* (or *dividing of time*). In addition to the scripture we've previously discussed (Dan 7:25), there are also these two:

*And I heard the man clothed in linen, which was upon the waters of the river, when he held up his right hand and his left hand unto heaven, and sware by him that liveth for ever that it shall be for **a time, times, and an half**; and when he shall have accomplished to scatter the power of the holy people, all these things shall be finished* (Dan 12:7)

*And to the woman were given two wings of a great eagle, that she might fly into the wilderness, into her place, where she is nourished for **a time, and times, and half a time**, from the face of the serpent* (Rev 12:14).

[As an aside, *scattering the power of the holy people* in Daniel 12:7 sure doesn't sound like a rapture has taken place. But keep your finger on Revelation 12:14, we're going to come back and revisit that hopeful verse again in due time.]

The word *time* is translated from the Aramaic word, *iddân,* meaning a *year.* King Nebuchadnezzar was given a prophecy that he would eat grass like an ox for *seven times* (or, as it happened, *seven years*; Dan 4:32). Thus, time = one year; times = two more years; half a time = half a year. Total them up and you get *three and a half years.*

The *time, times and half a time* corresponds to the final three and a half years that constitute the Great Tribulation. God uses variations of this phrase, but they always mean the same thing – The Great Tribulation: *42 months* (Rev 11:2; 13:5); and *1,260 days* (Rev 11:3, 12:6).

EARLY CHURCH KNEW THE TRUTH

The early Church fathers, many of whom were only one or two generations away from Christ and the Apostles, were unanimous in teaching that the Antichrist persecutes the Church and that the rapture occurs afterwards. The following quotes are compiled from Charles Cooper's excellent teaching on the Pre-Wrath Rapture Position:

The man of Apostacy [Antichrist]...*shall venture to do unlawful deeds on the earth against us the Christians.*
—Justin Martyr (c. 100-168)

Those, therefore, who continue steadfast, and are put through the fire, will be purified by means of it...Wherefore cease not speaking these things into the ears of the saints. This then is the type of the great tribulation that is yet to come.
—The Pastor of Hermes (c. 40-140)

And they [the Ten Kings of Revelation]...*shall give their kingdom to the beast, and put the church to flight...But* [John] *indicates the number of the name* [Antichrist, 666] *now, that when this man comes we may avoid him, being aware who he is.*
—Irenaeus (c. 140-200)

Now concerning the tribulation of the persecution which is to fall upon the Church from the adversary [speaking of Antichrist and his persecution of saints]...*That refers to the one thousand two hundred and threescore days* [the three and a half years of Great Tribulation] *during which the tyrant is to reign and persecute the Church.*
—Hippolytus (c. 160-240)

That the beast Antichrist with his false prophet may wage war on the Church of God...Since,

*then, the scriptures both indicate the stages of
the last times, and concentrate the harvest of the
Christian hope in the very end of the world.*
—Tertullian (c. 150-220)

THE QUESTION PRE-TRIBBERS
CAN'T ANSWER

Let's round out this chapter by presenting a question that
exposes the major flaw in the pre-tribulation rapture teaching.
It's a question I use whenever I'm discussing the rapture with
pre-tribulationists. And it's a question that they cannot
answer. Their inability to answer, much less understand the
concept, is the primary reason for their confusion about the
timing of the rapture. The question is this (see if you can
answer it):

Is there a difference between the Great Tribulation
and the Day of the Lord?

Most people simply lump these two events together as if
they were the same thing, happening at the same time. They
are *not!* And it's this particular misunderstanding of God's
word that most people cannot accurately and scripturally
determine the timing of the rapture of the saints and the
return of Jesus Christ. The Bible records the plan and outline
of end-time events in a chronological fashion, which
undeniably pinpoint the timing of the rapture and the return
of Christ. We will make this all plain as we proceed in this
book.

Regardless of the fact that most TV ministers promote
the pre-tribulation rapture, none can answer the question. Of
course, the reason is that if they *did* answer the question
correctly, they couldn't defend their pre-tribulation position
any longer. We will explain all this soon enough.

So if the scriptures do not present a pre-trib theology, and the early Church fathers did not promote a pre-trib theology, where did this teaching come from?

Pre-trib theology did not make its mark into the Church until the 1830s, when it was popularized by John Nelson Darby, a prominent Christian minister of the Plymouth Brethren, a Christian movement originating in Dublin, Ireland (according to Wikipedia entry for Darby). This fallacious theory may have died along with Darby when he passed away in 1882 but it received renewed interest once Cyrus Scofield incorporated this teaching into the liner notes of his Scofield Reference Bible, first published in 1909.

That book soon became a best-selling version of the Bible and has been used by countless theological seminaries since. And you don't get a seminary degree today without being exposed to teachings found in the Scofield Reference Bible.

Scofield's notes on the book of Revelation have been embraced by popular Christian pre-trib proponents, such as Hal Lindsey, Edgar C. Whisenant, Tim LaHaye, Jack Van Impe, and Chuck Missler. You have to look hard to find Christian leaders supporting any other position.

DON'T BE LEFT BEHIND IN KNOWLEDGE

The *Left Behind* movies and book series have continued to foster a false belief that God will rapture His Church before the Great Tribulation. But, as we've already seen, God has to cut short the Great Tribulation to preserve the elect of God and all human life. There's so much confusion over the end times that we need a little clarity about these issues lest we are *carried about by every wind of doctrine.*

So many people are so concerned about not being *left behind* in the rapture, they don't know they're being *left behind* in the knowledge and truth of the Word of God.

And then there are those who suggest that we're not even supposed to *understand* prophecy. But the book of Daniel says that at the time of the end *the wise shall understand* (Dan 12:10). And while many believe that the book of Revelation is a closed book, the first verse says it is *the revelation of Jesus Christ to show onto His servants things that must shortly come to pass* before the end of the age.

Let's take a fresh look at this subject and be like the Bereans of Acts 17:11, who even when none less than the Apostle Paul addressed them, would check everything he said by referring back to the scriptures – to see whether it was true or not. Let's not believe anyone's word carelessly – not even this author's. Let's look anew at the end-time scriptures that we may obtain a deeper understanding of the Great Tribulation, the Day of the Lord and the Church of the End Times.

What exactly is the Great Tribulation? Is it the same as the Day of the Lord?

We're going to lay out a sound argument that these two end-time events are *not* the same thing and it is this confusion, that they're both the same, that has led to no end of misunderstanding about the rapture. But once we understand the difference, we will be able to pinpoint the rapture. It's so simple, you'll be able to teach it.

So let's try to understand in a way that cannot be contradicted. And to do that we have to go step by step, verse by verse in a chronological fashion. For instance, if someone traveled from New York to Texas, he would have to follow landmarks or towns along the way. Therefore, Nashville, Tennessee, cannot come before Harrisburg, Pennsylvania. It's impossible in a direct route. The same can be said of how many today haphazardly connect landmarks on God's eschatological timetable. And this is why there is so much confusion. So, let us travel across God's prophetic end-time scenario and notice the beautiful symmetry in the landmarks along the way so that our course is clear, direct and without contradiction.

We're going to start at the beginning and work our way through, building a strong spinal column of major eschatological truths, from which, in time, minor points (even questionable matters) can subsequently be attached. Some might want to begin at Christ's famous Olivet Prophecy, but Christ, in fact, refers us back to Daniel (Mt 24:15). In effect, He's saying, "If you want to know about the end times, read and understand Daniel!" And, that's where we will begin. We will find that Daniel, Revelation and Christ's Olivet Prophecy are inextricably intertwined together. Daniel is incredibly important for its 70 Week prophecy, as it lays out for us the length of time that the end-time prophecies in Revelation and Christ's accounts require for fulfillment.

This bears repeating. While the end times have been upon us in a metaphorical sense since Christ walked the earth, we will make the case that the actual end times, as prophesied in Daniel (and other prophetic end-time scriptures), is only seven years long. If you keep this in mind, you'll be able to avoid the many pitfalls that beset many end-time prognosticators.

2
70 WEEK PROPHECY & CHRIST

Imagine your nation was chosen by God to be exceptional and a "beacon of light" to all other nations but *suddenly* it was reduced to third-world poverty status. In fact, your whole nation has been ransacked, defeated and taken over by the Babylonian Empire.

The once great God-fearing nation is reduced to servitude to a Gentile, idol-worshipping power. The year was circa 539 BC. The nation was Judah. The prophet trying to make sense of it all was Daniel, who was far from Jerusalem in Babylonian captivity.

Daniel sought answers from the God he served and was delighted when he was led to an earlier prophecy by a contemporary of his, the prophet Jeremiah, who said that the Babylonian captivity would be for a period of 70 years.

> *For thus saith the LORD, That after seventy years be accomplished at Babylon I will visit you, and perform my good word toward you, in causing you to return to this place* (Jer 29:10).

Great! Judah's captivity was coming to a close, so he thought. Seventy years were coming to an end, so he thought.

Then he'd be able to return back to Judah, so he thought. But details – *details!* – are needed here.

Daniel decided to seek the Lord in prayer about this prophecy and Judah's future. Yes, the Jewish captives would return back to Judah after 70 years. But, shockingly, at just about the time that the 70 years was up, Babylon falls to a succeeding power, the Medo-Persian empire. And, Judah is still in captivity! This exchange of rulers over Judah dismayed the prophet. More details are needed. And the details came by the Archangel Gabriel.

What we're going to explain today is an important prophecy given to Daniel that not only proves the Messiahship of Jesus Christ but also spans millennia to reach into our pulsating present day with its ultimate prophetic fulfillment for the end times. For God's answer is as relevant to the 21st century world as it was to Judah in the sixth century BC; in fact *it's even more so.*

Gabriel's message, which we will detail here, is contained in four distinct scriptures that we normally call *The 70 Week Prophecy.* Interestingly enough, this prophecy shows us both the beginning and the eternal victory of the Messiah, along with the beginning and the fall of the Anti-Messiah, or the Antichrist, after which the Kingdom of God reigns upon the earth forevermore.

We'll take these four scriptures one by one:

> **Seventy weeks** *are decreed as to your people and as to your holy city, to finish the transgression and to make an end of sins, and to make atonement for iniquity, and to bring in everlasting righteousness, and to seal up the vision and prophecy, and to anoint the Most Holy* (Dan 9:24, Modern King James Version).

Daniel was initially anticipating the end of Judah's 70 years captivity, but now Gabriel decrees *another* 70 Weeks on top of that 70! As we've seen in Chapter One, a *time,* in biblical parlance, is a period of *one year*. So too, now, Seventy Weeks has a biblical mathematical principle as well. Ezekiel 4:6 shows us that God uses a *day for a year* principle when calculating prophecy to be fulfilled. Each prophetic day is actually a year in duration. So what God is saying is that there will be another seventy weeks of seven (days), or 70 x 7, which equals 490 years.

These prophetic 490 years are determined upon God's people and upon Jerusalem, with the ultimate goal to:

- finish the nation's transgression
- make an end of sin
- make an atonement for iniquity
- bring in everlasting righteousness
- fulfill (seal up) the vision and prophecy
- anoint the Most Holy Place, which is the Holy of Holies in the Temple of God.

Notice the emphasis on sin and God graciously offering an atonement for sin. Judah found itself in captivity because of its sin and rebellion against God. They should have learned of sin's consequences from Israel, their sister nation to the north. For the sin of idolatry, Israel in the 8th century BC was conquered, ejected from their land and disappeared into the world — where they remain as lost tribes to this day.

The *atonement for iniquity* (sin) is certainly an allusion to Jesus, the Messiah, who would also *anoint* the Most Holy Place by His very presence in the Temple. This could only take place in the prophesied millennial reign of the Messiah, in the Kingdom of God, upon His return.

Therefore, the fulfillment of these 70 weeks coincides with the Messiah taking His rightful place as King over the earth.

But when does this span of time start? And where are we now in its fulfillment? And what does this have to do with today? Let's continue with the next verse.

TIMING OF THE MESSIAH'S APPEARANCE

Know therefore and understand, that from the going out of the command to restore and to build Jerusalem, to Messiah the Prince, shall be seven weeks, and sixty-two weeks. The street shall be built again, and the wall, even in times of affliction (Dan 9:25, MKJV).

Gabriel lays out the first 69 weeks of the prophecy, which he says begins when the *decree is issued to rebuild Jerusalem* and it ends when *the Messiah appears.* He breaks down this timeframe as 7 + 62 weeks, or a total of 69 weeks. Prophetically speaking, using *the day for a year* principle, that means 69 x 7 (for seven days in a week) equals 483 years.

So Jerusalem, though it was ransacked by the Babylonians and left in ruins, is going to be rebuilt!

Earlier we desired details and here they are. The fulfillment of Jeremiah's 70 years prophecy when the Jews would return to Jerusalem actually coincides with the beginning of Daniel's 70 Week Prophecy, when a decree is issued to rebuild the city.

At that time, God raised up a man named Nehemiah, who, conveniently enough, was cup-bearer to the Persian King Artaxerxes. The cup-bearer would guard against poison in the king's cup and was sometimes required to swallow the wine before serving it! This type of confidential relationship gave the cup-bearer great influence with the king. In the book of Nehemiah, we read about the decree to rebuild Jerusalem:

And it came to pass in the month Nisan, in the twentieth year of Artaxerxes the king, when wine was before him, that I took up the wine, and gave it unto the king. Now I had not been beforetime sad in his presence. And the king said unto me, Why is thy *countenance sad, seeing thou art not sick? this is nothing else but sorrow of heart. Then I was very sore afraid. And I said unto the king, Let the king live for ever: why should not my countenance be sad, when the city, the place of my fathers' sepulchres, lieth waste, and the gates thereof are consumed with fire? Then the king said unto me, For what dost thou make request? So I prayed to the God of heaven. And I said unto the king, **If it please the king, and if thy servant have found favour in thy sight, that thou wouldest send me unto Judah, unto the city of my fathers' sepulchres, that I may build it.** And the king said unto me, (the queen also sitting by him,) For how long shall thy journey be? and when wilt thou return? So it pleased the king to send me; and I set him a time. Moreover I said unto the king, If it please the king, let letters be given me to the governors beyond the river, that they may let me pass through till I come unto Judah; and a letter unto Asaph the keeper of the king's forest, that he may give me timber to make beams for the gates of the castle which appertaineth to the house, and for the wall of the city, and for the house that I shall enter into. And the king granted me, according to the good hand of my God upon me* (Neh 2:1-8).

Here we have the beginning date when the decree was issued. It was in the month of Nisan in the 20th year of Artaxerxes' reign. According to Jewish chronologies, when the day of the month is not given, it can be assumed that the first day is meant. Thus, the 1st of Nisan, in the 20th year of King Artaxerxes of Babylon corresponds to March 14, 445 BC (according to the website, Khouse.org, founded by Chuck and Nancy Missler).

Let's add 483 years to 445 BC and — *voila!* — converted to the Western calendar and corrected for leap years, we arrive at April 6, 32 AD!

THE TRIUMPHANT ENTRY

You tell me. Which Messianic figure was in the world in Spring 32 AD?

From the issuance of the decree to rebuild Jerusalem until the Messiah would be 483 years! That brings us right to the triumphant entry of Jesus Christ to Jerusalem just before His crucifixion for the world's sins!

Incidentally, Daniel's phrase "Messiah the Prince" in the King James translation is actually the Hebrew phrase, *Meshiach Nagid,* meaning "The Messiah the King."

This sure fulfillment of prophecy to prove the validity of God's Word and the power of Almighty God in world affairs is an indictment against our educational system which has expelled both God and His Word from students' curriculum! If only we can return back to a biblical world view, we'd see God's hand in every aspect of history and in our lives!

THE MESSIAH WOULD BE CRUCIFIED

The prophecy of Jesus continues in Daniel:

> *And after sixty-two weeks Messiah shall be cut off, but not for Himself. And the people of the ruler who shall come shall destroy the city and the sanctuary. And the end of it shall be with the flood, and ruins are determined, until the end shall be war* (Dan 9:26, MKJV).

Notice the accuracy of God's Word and the precision of its timing. Gabriel's word to Daniel not only pinpointed the timing of the Messiah's appearance, but *now* it also tells us that He would be crucified: *Messiah shall be cut off, but not for Himself.*

The phrase, *not for Himself,* means He died for the sins of the world. The Judeo-Christian theology of sin is *real.* The consequences of sin *are* evident all around us in this evil world we live in. But the sacrifice for sins was paid in *full* by Jesus Christ.

It is never too late to turn to Him in humility and to ask Him to take away our sins so that we can have eternal life of joy and fulfillment with Him in this world and in the world to come. The only afterlife reality we can expect is what Jesus tells us about heaven and hell.

Now the prophetic word continues: *And the people of the ruler who shall come shall destroy the city and the sanctuary.* Jerusalem would by this time be no longer ruled over by the Persians, but by the Romans. And, sure enough, history shows us that after the Crucifixion of Jesus Christ, Roman armies came into Jerusalem and sacked the city and destroyed the Temple in 70 AD.

Jesus warned his followers that destruction was coming to both the Temple (*not one stone shall be upon another that shall not be cast down*, Mt 24:2) and to Jerusalem (*O Jerusalem, Jerusalem, which killeth the prophets, and stoneth them that are sent unto her! how often would I have gathered thy children together, even as a hen gathereth her chickens under her wings, and ye would not! Behold, your house is left unto you desolate,* Mt 23:37-38).

The phrase in Daniel, *And the end of it shall be with the flood,* recalls the biblical idiom using the word *flood* to denote marauding armies overrunning the land (Isa 28:1-2).

The destruction to Jerusalem and of the Temple in 70 AD were mere prototypes of what will occur again during the last week of Daniel's 70 Week prophecy, when the Temple will be rebuilt for the Antichrist.

Now we turn to the phrase, *ruins are determined, until the end shall be war.* This too, prophetically, has been fulfilled. For many centuries, Jerusalem had been left in ruins and the city had been the center of conflicts and wars since then.

So we've seen how God fulfilled his prophecy up till now. But that's only 69 weeks! There's another scripture to go. What happens to the "last week" of Daniel? When does that begin?

The last week outlined in "Daniel's 70 Weeks" jumps us prophetically to our pulsating 21st century. This ancient prophecy given to Daniel by the Archangel Gabriel offers us clues to the identity of the Antichrist and gives us pronouncements of tomorrow's news.

3
70 WEEK PROPHECY & ANTICHRIST

Now we come to a very important prophetic word that is relevant to our day and time! It is the scripture that Jesus told his followers to refer to in order to understand the end-time scenario. It's going to identify the Antichrist to come and determine the length of time for *all things to be fulfilled.*

There is much speculation and confusion about the Antichrist, so it's important to not be deceived by every *wind of doctrine* (Eph 4:14) that has and will come along. Jesus repeatedly emphasized that His people not be deceived about the Signs of the Times heralding His return (Mt 24:4-5, 11, 23-26).

After 69 prophetic weeks have come and gone, with a large lapse of time since the completion of the 69th week, Daniel's prophecy gives us a clue as to when that important and final 70th week begins. And when it begins, we will have *seven more years* before the return of Jesus Christ. In Daniel's last prophetic week of seven years, we will see *all things* prophesied for the end times to be *fulfilled within that time frame!*

Are we close to that last *seven years?* Of course, we are. And with each and every day, we're closer still.

We may be so close to that prophetic week of *seven years* that we wouldn't be surprised if the Antichrist is already alive on earth, waiting unseen in the wings for his debut performance. We'll discuss this further in the next chapter.

ONE EVENT – ONLY ONE! – THAT TRIGGERS THE LAST SEVEN YEARS

The irony is that while there is such an increased anticipation of the end times, yet with our being so woefully ignorant of eschatology, we find ourselves constantly bombarded by prognosticators' false-alarm signs of His return. With precision speed, every event we see in the news today seems to trigger someone to declare, "We're in the end times! America is being judged! This President is the Antichrist!" People get so rattled from hearing this constant mishmash of scripture that it'd be great if we had some balance and discernment.

But here's good news. **Once you understand this basic principle, you will realize that the last seven years is triggered by *one event* and *one event only.*** So you can push aside every other false concept that panics you into stockpiling food, intimidates you from advancing Kingdom, prevents you from carrying out exploits for the Lord, and dashes your hopes to fulfill your destiny.

Here then is Daniel's *last week* prophetic word. (Jesus' Olivet Prophecy affirms that the "he" spoken of in the following is that of the Antichrist.)

> *And he shall confirm the covenant with many for one week: and in the midst of the week he shall cause the sacrifice and the oblation to cease, and for the overspreading of abominations he shall make it*

desolate, even until the consummation, and that determined shall be poured upon the desolate (Dan 9:27).

Let's first understand what this is *not* saying!

- Nowhere does it say that the *covenant* is a *peace treaty,* as many contend;
- Nowhere does it say that the covenant is *proposed* as a *seven year* covenant. God is merely telling us that it will only *last* seven years, until Christ's return, as fulfillment of Daniel's last week prophecy.

Here's what it *does* tell us.

- Jerusalem is still the focal point for this prophecy, since the entire 70 Week prophecy has to do with Jerusalem (Dan 9:2);
- The Antichrist will *confirm the covenant* there — but *what* covenant?

We find that other bible translations say he *will enforce a covenant* (Holman Christian Standard Bible) or *strengthen a covenant* (Young's Literal Translation).

Thus we see that one will come on the scene *confirming, enforcing,* or *strengthening* a covenant (apparently, an *already* "established" covenant — since you can't *enforce* or *strengthen* a covenant that wasn't there before!).

CONFIRMING THE COVENANT — WHAT JEWS ARE SAYING

We must remember that the Jews of today, having rejected Jesus as their Messiah, are still looking for the One to fulfill the scriptures pertaining to Messiah. Jesus remonstrated with the Jews:

I am come in my Father's name, and ye receive me not: if another shall come in his own name, him ye will receive (Jn 5:43).

Furthermore, while the next verse is a reference to Christ's *second* coming to establish the Millennium, the Jews today apply this to the *first* appearance of the Messiah.

Behold, the days come, saith the LORD, that I will make a new covenant with the house of Israel, and with the house of Judah (Jer 31:31).

Let's see how modern Jewish thinkers understand the *new covenant:*

> *"It is evident that Jeremiah's use of the term 'a new covenant' does not involve the replacement of the (eternal) Torah by the New Testament. Rather, it signals a renewal of the original Sinai Covenant."*
>
> — Uri Yosef, PhD (article, "Will the Real New Covenant Please Stand Up?")

> *"Jeremiah's 'new covenant' is not a replacement of the existing covenant, but merely a figure of speech expressing the reinvigoration and revitalization of the existing covenant."*
>
> — JewsforJudaism.org

So that means that when someone comes *reestablishing or reaffirming the covenant*, the Jews will be ready to embrace him.

In other words, when the Antichrist *confirms the covenant* — actually *renews* the covenant of old (complete with the animal sacrifices and the rebuilding of the Temple) – he will be accepted by the Jews of today!

Let's continue in Daniel, keeping that context in mind. We will see that this verse has everything to do with the Antichrist reinstituting animal sacrifices and then disbanding them – placing himself as god in the Temple. This is confirmed once you continue the scripture.

> *And he shall confirm the covenant with many for one week: and in the midst of the week he shall cause the sacrifice and the oblation to cease* (Dan 9:27).

The scripture is telling us quite plainly that the two lines in verse 27 are connected. Antichrist *confirms the covenant* for seven years (which reinstitutes animal sacrifices in Jerusalem), then in the middle of the seven years he *breaks the covenant* involving animal sacrifices!

Whether the Temple in Jerusalem is already built at the time of the *confirming of the covenant* or not remains to be seen. But this scripture is telling us so much more than we realize.

SEVEN YEAR PEACE TREATY – NOT!

Many people believe that the Antichrist confirms a *peace treaty* in the Middle East. But we know of no Bible translation that adds the word *peace* to this scripture. In fact, as we will read later on in the chapter on "Antichrist wars," he is anything but a peacemonger.

Rather, the answer is contained within the scripture itself. Notice the conformity of the two clauses in the phrase, inferring that the Antichrist confirms a covenant on the one hand and then breaks it by ending the sacrifices and oblations. In fact, as we know from other scriptures, what begins as a call to reestablish the greatness of Israel suddenly, when the "man of sin" is revealed midpoint (2 Thess 2:3), morphs into a demand to worship Antichrist (Rev 13:8).

THE ANTICHRIST IS NOT ISLAMIC!

We have a tendency to believe that the Antichrist is going to forcibly impose his authority upon Israel against its will. Perhaps it's a result of recent teachings that the Antichrist will be Islamic. But no. Israel will welcome the false messiah, and he will be one of their own, as we've seen in John 5:43.

The Jews are, after all, still awaiting their messiah, one who will establish the greatness of Israel's national identity and defeat their foes (Acts 1:6, Ps 110:1-7).

Furthermore, the Antichrist will present a façade of "righteousness" in leading the nation of Israel to ritualistic animal sacrifices in a feigned atonement for sin. Then suddenly in the middle of the seven years, he abruptly morphs the worship towards himself.

Not understanding these points has led many to assume various political leaders who carry the attributes of Antichrist to be the final Antichrist. John has shown us that there are *many antichrists* already in the world, but there will be only one final Antichrist (1 Jn 2:18).

But is the final Antichrist Islamic? Many Christians have latched onto this idea recently due to the worldwide rise of Christian martyrs by Islamic terrorists. This is compounded by the rise of Christians being misled into combining end-time teachings of the Bible with the Koran. This is a dangerous precedent that will certainly mislead many down a road of confusion.

Perhaps without meaning to, they are trying to prove the reliability of the Holy Scripture by using the Koran as supplementary support. They are creating a type of *Chrislamization of Eschatology.*

Scripture says, *To the Law and to the testimony! If they do not speak according to **this** Word, it is because no light is in them* (Isa 8:20, MKJV; cp 2 Cor 6:14). We shouldn't be trying to force non-biblical beliefs into the Word of God.

But let's see just how problematic an Islamic Antichrist is to the realities of Middle Eastern sensibilities. We know that the religious Jews in the Middle East are awaiting their Messiah. Would the Jews embrace one who comes in the name of Islam as the leader of a religion that seeks the *destruction* of Israel? The Jews have been conditioned since their Nation's inception to protect themselves from their Arab neighbors all around them. Time after time, the Israelis have sought peace with the Palestinians and surrounding Arab nations, only to become the object of their hatred and scorn. Does it sound logical that the Jews will now accept an Islamic Messiah?

Conversely, would the adherents of Islam support an Islamic leader over the Jews, one who wouldn't be imposing Sharia Law on them? Rather, this supposed Islamic Messiah must, according to scripture, be actively renewing God's covenant with Israel — thus subjugating and making inferior the religion of Islam to that of the Jews! How many Muslims would accept that? How many more would revolt against it?

More problems: Jesus makes it clear that many will be deceived in the end times. What would happen if the Antichrist *were* Islamic? The answer is plain — many Christians would quickly denounce him as Antichrist. But suppose he comes as a Jewish hero warrior, re-instituting the Old Covenant, rebuilding the Temple and defeating Israel's terrorist neighbors? How many well-meaning supporters of Israel – many Christians, in fact – would fall for that scenario? Many will. And yet, that's the scenario to come.

Think this through. If the end-time Antichrist is Islamic, every Christian would be able to spot that fraud from a mile away. They couldn't possibly be deceived. But suppose that the Antichrist is Jewish, defending the State of Israel and defeating all her Arab terrorist neighbors? How many well-meaning Christians in America and the West would have a knee-jerk reaction supporting this Jewish leader? The Western Christian church has been conditioned for decades to support Israel at all costs! This is why Christ constantly warned His followers to not be deceived.

Meanwhile, the Jewish scholars who are still awaiting the Messiah will no doubt look to the scriptures for verification of the "Messiah's" appearance and they will give their allegiance to him.

They will be looking for one who will once again restore Jerusalem's greatness. This is what they expect the Messiah to do. Remember, this is the very thing that the disciples asked of Jesus in Acts 1:6 (*"Will you now restore the Kingdom to Israel?"*).

Now let's review Daniel 9:27, for this scripture gives us three unmovable landmarks to help us understand the timeline of Daniel's 70th Week.

1. **How long are the end times?** Daniel's last week tells us it's only seven years. All of the eschatological scriptures fall into this seven year period! Knowing this, we can better lay out end-time scriptures for our seven year timeline. Today Christians have the authority and right to pray for national awakening and revival in accordance with God's will. But once this period begins, there is no way to pray against these prophesied events, as all scripture must be fulfilled. This is a landmark point, and, once it begins, nothing can pray this away.

2. **When does Daniel's last week of seven years begins?** Antichrist reaffirms the covenant of animal sacrifices and Temple worship in Jerusalem! Don't let anyone confuse you about when the last seven years begin. Many have looked to the constellations in the sky to determine when this period begins. They look to asteroids, imaginary Planet X's. Many were fooled by the so-called constellation of Revelation 12 during September 2017. Do not be fooled. God gives us here the only defining event that begins the last seven years.

3. **What begins the Great Tribulation?** Antichrist ends
   the animal sacrifices at midpoint (3 ½ years into the
   last seven years) and enters the Temple, demanding
   worship from the world.

This is all so very simple: three immutable landmarks.
Let's keep this firmly in mind as we continue mapping out the
events in the last days, because it's crucial to lay this down as
the foundation for our understanding.

THE ABOMINATION THAT CAUSES DESOLATION

We've seen that Daniel's last prophesied week is composed
of seven years. At the beginning of the seven years — *and
this is how* ***you will know when*** *the seven years begins!* —
the one who will become the Antichrist renews the Old
Covenant, reestablishing the Temple and the animal
sacrifices. Then three and a half years later, in the middle of
the week, the animal sacrifices are abruptly terminated, and
that begins the Great Tribulation.

> *And he shall confirm the covenant with many for one
> week: and in the midst of the week he shall cause the
> sacrifice and the oblation to cease, and for the
> overspreading of abominations he shall make it
> desolate, even until the consummation, and that
> determined shall be poured upon the desolate* (Dan
> 9:27).

The New International Version explains the latter part of
the verse better than the King James Version:

> *And at the temple he will set up an abomination that
> causes desolation, until the end that is decreed is
> poured out on him* (Dan 9:27, NIV).

The abomination that is set up is the Antichrist's demand for worship in the Temple. *He* is the abomination, which makes Jerusalem *desolate!* For the destruction of Jerusalem is spurred by *his* actions. Jesus, foretelling Armageddon, says:

> *And when ye shall see Jerusalem compassed with armies, then know that the **desolation** thereof is nigh* (Lk 21:20).

But before the Antichrist is *destroyed by the brightness of (Christ's) coming* (2 Thess 2:8), Jesus explains to His disciples (and *us!*) the immediate ramifications of Antichrist's demand for worship.

> *Therefore when you see the abomination of desolation, spoken of by Daniel the prophet, stand in the holy place (whoever reads, let him understand). Then let those in Judea flee into the mountains. Let him on the housetop not come down to take anything out of his house; nor let him in the field turn back to take his clothes. And woe to those who are with child, and to those who give suck in those days! But pray that your flight is not in the winter, nor on the sabbath day; **for then shall be great tribulation,** such as has not been since the beginning of the world to this time; no, nor ever shall be. And unless those days should be shortened, no flesh would be saved. But for the elect's sake, those days shall be shortened* (Mt 24:15-22, MKJV, also compare 2 Thess 2:3-4).

Jesus tells us that once Antichrist demands worship, that is the start of the Great Tribulation!

At the risk of being repetitious, let's once more put this into perspective and right alignment.

***You will know* the start of the Daniel's last seven years when Antichrist confirms a covenant that reinstitutes the animal sacrifices, which lasts for three and a half years!**

Then, at the midpoint of the seven years, *you will know* **the start of the final three and a half years when Antichrist stops the animal sacrifices and demands worship for himself .**

The Great Tribulation will technically last for three and a half years. We say *technically* because the Great Tribulation is so horrific that God, in His mercy, *cuts it short by His return!* Notice, Jesus' statement: *And unless those days (the Great Tribulation) should be shortened, no flesh would be saved (alive). But for the elect's sake, those days shall be shortened* (Mt 24:22).

This is why no one knows *the day or the hour* **of His return! Even though we may know the exact** *watch of the night* **and the exact** *time and season* **for His return. Even though we will definitely know when we're in the last seven years and definitely know the exact day that the Great Tribulation starts. But we will not know the exact** *day or hour* **when Christ cuts short the Great Tribulation for His return!**

While we do not know by how much those three and a half years will be cut short (maybe by a year?), we do know that once it is cut, it begins the Day of the Lord and the return of Christ. We will explain all this in due time. We're first building our foundation and we will see how it all falls perfectly in line with scripture.

WHAT IS ABOMINATION TO GOD?

In concluding this chapter, it is interesting to do a word study on what God views as *abomination* and you'll find it has all the hallmark characteristics of the Antichrist:

> *Lying lips are abomination to the LORD: but they that deal truly are his delight* (Prov 12:22)

> *The sacrifice of the wicked is an abomination to the*

LORD: but the prayer of the upright is his delight. The way of the wicked is an abomination unto the LORD: but he loveth him that followeth after righteousness (Prov 15:8-9)

The thoughts of the wicked are an abomination to the LORD: but the words of the pure are pleasant words (Prov 15:26)

Every one that is proud in heart is an abomination to the LORD: though hand join in hand, he shall not be unpunished (Prov 16:5)

It is an abomination to kings to commit wickedness: for the throne is established by righteousness (Prov 16:12)

He that justifieth the wicked, and he that condemneth the just, even they both are abomination to the LORD (Prov 17:15).

Ultimately, when Christ returns to the New Jerusalem, God makes it a point to not allow in anyone who *worketh abomination:*

And there shall in no wise enter into it any thing that defileth, neither whatsoever worketh abomination, or maketh a lie: but they which are written in the Lamb's book of life (Rev 21:27).

Next chapter, we'll see why there is no predetermined start date for the last seven years. God alone, in His wisdom, will determine when that begins, as He empowers His people now to fulfill their "finest hour" before His return.

4
SEALS ON WHEELS

Facebook and other social media venues seem to have spawned hundreds of dime-store prognosticators, each vying for the singular position of pinpointing the exact day and time that the rapture takes place. Others seem to enjoy citing various and sundry current events as the pivotal moment that ignites Daniel's last week!

Many specific rapture dates have come and gone. If you missed one, don't worry. Another is right behind it. Blood moons and asteroids and comets have come and gone. The World Trade Center destruction was supposed to signal America was Babylon and judgment has come upon her; each new U.S. President has been tagged as the Antichrist; etc, etc, blah, blah, blah.

Needless to say, we are so confused and ignorant of Bible facts. Yet if you've read the last chapter, you know there is only *one event* to look for that begins the prophetic countdown to the return of Christ! Daniel 9:27 tells us it's when Antichrist confirms a covenant in Jerusalem reestablishing Temple worship. *That's it!* Don't look for asteroids in the sky. Don't look for rapture dates given by YouTube sensations.

Then why haven't we been taught this simple truth? For a number of reasons, but let's focus on one. Most of the Church ignores Daniel's prophetic countdown marker and instead bases its end-time calculations on a flawed understanding of scripture, which they feel is talking about the modern state of Israel.

WRONG INTERPRETATION

We have been taught that Jesus was referring to the establishment of the state of Israel in 1948 when He said,

> *Now learn a parable of the fig tree; When his branch is yet tender, and putteth forth leaves, ye know that summer is nigh: So likewise ye, when ye shall see all these things, know that it is near, even at the doors* (Mt 24:32-33).

They say that the fig tree was always symbolic of Israel and that when Israel became a state, the countdown had begun.

And we've believed that. Yet no one ever seems to go to Luke's account of the Olivet Prophecy to find that Jesus was not referring to the state of Israel at all. Luke says,

> *And he spake to them a parable; Behold the fig tree, and **all the trees*** (Lk 21:29).

Notice He was not singling out the fig tree or Israel. He was referencing the fig tree and *all* trees! He was simply emphasizing the speed in which all these things should come to pass, as quickly as seasons come and go. Continuing with this important verse in Matthew, Jesus says:

> ***This generation shall not pass, till all these things be fulfilled*** (Mt 24:34).

How long is a *generation*? Ever since 1948 we've been fudging around with that number. We've so tried to fit the scripture into our beliefs that we've been extending the length of a biblical *generation* in *every* generation – from 20 years, to 40 years, to 70 years (and we'll likely go beyond that, should the Lord tarry)!

So we've been misled on this and a number of important prophecies. Yet the Lord has given us precise instruction that will define the generation that will see all these things come to pass! It'll not be 70 years duration, it'll not be 40, and it'll not be 20. It'll be *swift* and catch many unawares.

The scriptures speak of a seven year timeline: it's correct, it's unchangeable — and, unfortunately, we've not been taught this. **So when Jesus says *this generation shall not pass till all these things be fulfilled*, He was referring to Daniel's last seven years.**

We're spending considerable time on this timeline because this is the *backbone* to which we attach every other end-time prophetic event in a chronological fashion. The timing of the rapture is *dependent* upon this timeline, as is the clear distinction between the Great Tribulation and the Day of the Lord. This timeline houses both the Seven Seals of Revelation and Christ's Olivet Prophecy, which we will explain in the next few chapters.

By the time readers finish this book, they will walk away with both a greater understanding of end-time events (with a greater specificity than they've had before) and a deeper sense of God's intelligent design in the scriptures, as we marvel how precisely scripture fits into this biblical timeline.

The book of Daniel is the most important prophetic book of the Old Testament, whose prophecies catapult the reader to its fulfillment in the days we're living in now. We'll soon see how Daniel fits so well with Revelation and Christ's own words.

For review, here are some bullet points to consider about the 70 week prophecy (Dan 9:25-27):

- God determined 70 weeks to fulfill His plan for the restoration of Jerusalem and His coming Kingdom
- The 70 weeks, using the day for a year principle (Ezek 4:6), prophetically became 490 years
- The first 69 weeks (or 483 years) precisely pinpoint the timeframe, beginning with the pronouncement to rebuild the city of Jerusalem (445 BC) until the crucifixion of the Messiah (32 AD) (as converted to the Western calendar and adjusted for leap years)
- That last week of seven years *begins* with the appearance of the Antichrist and *ends* with the return of the Messiah
- **The last week of seven years duration has been held in suspension, by God's discretion, until an appointed time yet in our future, hopefully in our lifetimes**

SEVEN YEARS ON WHEELS

The beauty of this last seven years is that the Lord in His infinite wisdom can place this uninterrupted period of seven years anywhere He wishes on the world's calendar. And, it may very well be determined when the "fullness of the Gentiles" is complete (Rom 11:25). God, and *only* God, can determine when is the best time to initiate these crucial last seven years of the world's system, and the beginning of His Kingdom reign on earth.

Since God requires the participation of the Saints in God's end-time work, this gives Him flexibility to delay things until His bride is ready and the harvesting of souls

has reached its peak. Hence, it's seven years on wheels, so to speak: It's calendar adjustable!

It's not fixed to a prophetic starting date – it's fixed to an event! It's not something that will occur without notice – the world will see it on the news.

And *that* event can occur at any time, but only at the discretion of Father God (Mt 24:36).

Therefore, what is important to note is that this seven year period – just ahead of us now! – will encompass the fulfillment of the end-time prophesied events from the Bible! Using this key, we can begin to see how New Testament prophecies – including the Seals of Revelation – fit into this portable timeline of seven years, opening up to us a wealth of understanding!

GOD IS PREPARING A PEOPLE

Each year it seems reckless predictors of doom and gloom are causing great anxiety among God's people. For decades, even well known TV evangelists have continually set end-time dates as they are carelessly guided by blood moons and dire events on the earth. And to what profit? They've left in their wake a dispirited legacy of failed predictions, dashed hopes and unfulfilled destinies.

We've produced a culture within Christian circles where our only focus is on either escaping the world in a pre-tribulation rapture or hopelessly waiting for the next destructive shoe to drop all around us. Neither option has the heart of God in it.

These unnecessary distractions cause Christians to become disheartened from pursuing the call for which they've been put here on this earth. The importance of this book is to set us free from mindless speculations about the end times and to buck us up so that we fulfill our destinies and callings.

Each of us has been given a mandate from heaven to

accomplish – we're marked from birth with a clear purpose to fulfill His will. God has provided all we need to fulfill our calling. He's given us giftings, anointings, talents, direction, Holy-Spirit insight, and angels from on high to work out every detail of our commissioning.

The beauty of God's *Seals on Wheels* is that God can patiently prune his vine, cultivate its soil, and bring out the best in His people without rushing the process – for He knows our weaknesses. But already in the earth we are seeing a remnant arising that intimately knows their God and embraces the purposes for which they've been put here on earth. They've been trained to know God's Presence and to hear His voice in the secret place. And they shall carry the weighty glory of the Lord with powerful signs, wonders and miraculous healings, all the while performing the greatest exploits unparalleled in all human history.

I'm reminded of a prophetic dream the Lord gave me to encourage us about the days we're living in now. In my dream, I walked backstage at a Matt Sorger Christian conference and I glanced over and noticed the next guest speaker — he was British Prime Minister Winston Churchill (1874 – 1965). I was excited, thrilled and eager to meet him.

As I raced to embrace and welcome him to the conference, my mind was flooded with thankfulness for all he had done during World War II. If you recall history, Churchill, with his reassuring voice, emboldened his nation with words of faith and encouragement to fight against the menacing Nazis.

Adolf Hitler was taking over the whole of Europe during the darkest hours of World War II. Many nations had already fallen. Movie newsreels showed German soldiers and tanks surveilling their new war trophies – Paris' Eiffel Tower and the Arc De Triomphe. What a shock for the world to see France's fall to the Nazis. And now England was next to fall in the Nazi quest to control the world.

In some ways, the fear and dread people had then about

the Nazi advance into England is the same fear we have today about the Satanic advance into our culture. With each news report of doom and gloom and with each powerful wind blowing against our lamp, we can only seem to muster an expectation of the next shoe to drop – and no more.

But in World War II, there was a lone voice: Winston Churchill. And he turned the nation around. His lone voice inspired a nation not to give in to despair and to move forward with confidence to victory, despite overwhelming military power against them. His greatest phrase, which echoed in everyone's heart, was that this victory would be *their finest hour!*

So I shook his hand vigorously and a mighty tangible anointing of the Holy Spirit fell on us both.

When I awoke, I knew that Winston Churchill represented a legacy for today of those who would stand tall and speak out, encouraging and leading this present generation even though things get darker around us…and they will get darker…we, too, the remnant of Christians, will prevail in this *our finest hour!*

So even though things look ominous all around us, don't give up. Keep the faith. Advance the Kingdom. Heal the sick. Cleanse the lepers. Cast out the demonic.

This is the time in which we were specifically born to excel. If you're reading this now, this is your time. This is your hour. This is your mandate.

Amidst the upheaval in the world, God is preparing a worldwide awakening. Are we on board with that? Or are we seeking any excuse to shirk our duties by relying on doomsday prognosticators who are distracting us from our mission? Don't miss out on what God is presently doing on the earth. We already see God's hand in electing a "bulldozer," Donald J. Trump, against all odds, to become President of the United States. God has stopped America's freefall into oblivion by halting the satanic forces pushing globalization. God has a purpose for sparing America, defying all the doomsayers saying America's days are over. We can clearly see that Satan has been trying to prematurely push end-time events so as to prevent the mighty move of God to fill the earth! So God intervened on America's behalf to spawn a global awakening. And you and I are a part of this awesome spectacle. Let us seize the opportunity before us and freely work the fields of harvest.

When we're always rattled by every cry of doom, we're neglecting to advance His causes in our Nation. When we're seeking escape, it shows we're not concerned about the people we're leaving behind.

Rather than letting our destinies be sidetracked and robbed by a barrage of negative speculation, Jesus says for us to *occupy till He comes* (Lk 19:13). Let's take ground for Him now. God has positioned us to transform society around us. And we can do it if we focus our attentions to do so. The greatest outpouring of His Spirit is just ahead of us now. Let none of us miss out on our golden opportunity to reach our highest potential in Christ and fulfill our glorious destinies.

So now that we know the one sign God gives us that initiates the last seven years of this present world, we can disregard every other misleading proclamation and run the race without hindrance.

Imagine, on your watch, you can help turn a Nation around. That's our calling. That's our mandate. Rather than waiting for the next shoe to drop, you have time to pursue your destiny and calling and impact a nation. That way, this too, may be *your* finest hour! *Go for it!*

5
JESUS REVEALS THE SEALS

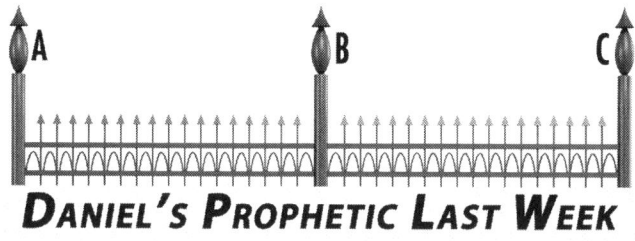

DANIEL'S PROPHETIC LAST WEEK

Now we're going to see how the end-time prophecies all fit into the timeline of Daniel's last seven years. At beginning point A, Antichrist initiates Temple worship in Israel. At midpoint B, Antichrist enters the Temple and demands worship from all. By the end of timeline C, Christ takes over the reigns of the earth.

Once we include what Jesus says at both the Olivet Prophecy and from the book Revelation, we will see that the period from A to B is called the *beginning of sorrows*, and the period from B to C is called the *Great Tribulation*. We've already discussed the fact that God, in His mercy and by His prerogative, *cuts short* the three and a half years of Great Tribulation by His return.

Now let's put some of the pieces together by going to the book of Revelation. We'll find that it is a chronological book overall, with certain inset chapters to deepen our understanding.

> *The Revelation of Jesus Christ which God gave unto him, to shew unto his servants things which must shortly come to pass* (Rev 1:1).

Notice the Revelation comes from Jesus Christ and not John the Apostle as is inferred by some translators in their naming of the book. We think of the book now as a mysterious "closed" book and incomprehensible, but Jesus says He gave John this Word to show his people *things to come.* Yes, Jesus *wants* to reveal things to us.

> *Blessed is he that readeth, and they that hear the words of this prophecy, and keep those things which are written therein: for the time is at hand* (Rev 1:3).

The Lord pronounces blessings upon all who *read* the book of Revelation, *hear* the prophecies written therein, and *keep* the prophecies in their heart (Rev 22:7).

Incidentally, for those who think that 70 AD fulfilled all prophecies in the Bible, please notice that the book of Revelation was written *after* the destruction of Jerusalem. It was written circa 90 AD by the aged patriarch John, who alone escaped martyrdom of all the apostles.

> *And I saw a strong angel proclaiming with a loud voice, Who is worthy to open the book, and to loose the seals thereof?* (Rev 5:2).

The prophecy which Father God gave to the Lord was originally a rolled up scroll affixed with seven seals. But it was meant to be opened and only Jesus was found worthy to open the scroll (Rev 1:3-5, 9). As each seal was removed, it released part of the prophecy in a chronological fashion. So each seal followed one another in sequential order.

Let's now give an overall summary of the Seven Seals of Revelation, after which we will go into detail.

- The first four seals are the four horsemen of the Apocalypse: and can be broken down as false Christs, war, famine and death
- The fifth seal is the Great Tribulation
- The sixth seal is the signs in the sun, moon, and stars
- The seventh seal is the Day of the Lord (Christ's return is combined with judgment, which is composed of Seven Trumpets, the seventh of which is composed of Seven Bowl Judgments)

Wait a second! If the four horsemen of the Apocalypse are *false Christs, wars, famine* and *death*, well, we've always had them on the world's scene. What sets these apart to designate the end times?

This is why Jesus instructed His disciples to refer to Daniel's timeline for insight about the last days. Daniel and the book of Revelation, along with Christ's Olivet Prophecy in Matthew 24, are three passages of scripture that compliment each other and need to be read together. We will find that once the Antichrist reaffirms Temple worship, it will begin the seven year timeline, which will cause a chain reaction that propels the next three horsemen of wars, famine and death to fully ride for the first three and a half years.

After reading the next set of bullet points, please *reread* them again. It's very important to keep these points in mind as a foundation to fully understand what is to follow:

- Each seal is closed until an appointed time
- Only Jesus was deemed worthy to open the seals
- Jesus opens one seal at a time
- That means the seals are released chronologically
- That means the seals cannot be moved or switched about from their precise chronology to fit a preconceived prophetic theory
- Each seal can only be opened during Daniel's prophetic last seven years
- The first four seals (the Four Horsemen) correspond to the period of time Jesus refers to as the *beginning of sorrows* (Mt 24:8), or the first half of Daniel's last seven years
- The last three seals correspond to the second half of Daniel's last seven years, which includes the Great Tribulation and the Day of the Lord
- You will notice that the fifth seal (Great Tribulation) is *not* the same as the seventh seal (Day of the Lord). They are *separated* by the sixth seal, which is the sign in the sun, moon and stars.

Not understanding the difference between the Great Tribulation and the Day of the Lord is the major cause for so much confusion in the Body of Christ, leading many into various interpretations for Christ's return. But once you understand the difference, there is no more confusion. More about that as we progress in this teaching.

Since Jesus has been found worthy to open the seals and becomes the Revelator, it is not surprising to find that Jesus also reveals the seals privately to His disciples while He was on the earth. We will, therefore, compare side by side the

JESUS REVEALS THE SEALS

seals in Revelation with Christ's comments in the Olivet Prophecy.

THE FIRST SEAL –
False Christs, Specifically the Antichrist

John the aged Apostle was invited to see, in a heavenly vision, the sequential opening of the seven seals from Father God's prophetic scroll. Jesus the Revelator peels open the first seal:

> *And I saw when the Lamb opened one of the seals, and I heard, as it were the noise of thunder, one of the four beasts saying, Come and see. And I saw, and behold a white horse: and he that sat on him had a bow; and a crown was given unto him: and he went forth conquering, and to conquer* (Rev 6:1-2).

Meanwhile, over in Matthew, the disciples came to Christ, just as you and I are now, to understand what shall happen in the last days. And Jesus was more than willing to have them understand.

> *And as he sat upon the mount of Olives, the disciples came unto him privately, saying, Tell us, when shall these things be? and what shall be the sign of thy coming, and of the end of the world? And Jesus answered and said unto them, Take heed that no man deceive you. For many shall come in my name, saying, I am Christ; and shall deceive many* (Mt 24:3-5).

The parallel between the two scriptures may not be immediately noticed. The verse in Revelation talks about a conqueror on a white horse, the second talks about false Christs who will deceive many. The two are *not* incompatible, though.

61

The spirit of Antichrist, which Jesus describes on the Mount of Olives, is actually the very spirit that operates within this military conqueror on a white horse. The Antichrist will, after all, be known as a *man of war* (Rev 13:4). We will devote much more time to the militaristic character of the Antichrist in a later chapter.

The Antichrist is pictured here as the one riding a *white horse*. He is the counterfeit Messiah, so he comes on a white horse conquering other nations, and ultimately the world – because, after all, so will the real Christ upon His second coming:

> *And I saw heaven opened, and behold a white horse; and he that sat upon him was called Faithful and True, and in righteousness he doth judge and make war … And out of his mouth goeth a sharp sword, that with it he should smite the nations: and he shall rule them with a rod of iron* (Rev 19:11, 15).

As we continue this study, we will find that Satan, who gives power to the Antichrist, allows him to literally die in order to be raised up again – in an apparent stunt to mimic the real resurrection of Christ (Rev 13:3-4).

Couple that with the demonic signs and wonders the Antichrist revels in and you can see that the Antichrist will try to imitate the real Christ in every way possible.

This is why Jesus was so adamant in warning His followers about not being deceived by false Christs – since *all* false Christs, *especially* the end-time Antichrist – would be so deceptive, convincing and damaging! (Mt 24:4-5).

THE SECOND SEAL –
Wars

> *And when he had opened the second seal, I heard the second beast say, Come and see. And there went out*

another horse that was red: and power was given to him that sat thereon to take peace from the earth, and that they should kill one another: and there was given unto him a great sword (Rev 6:3-4)

And ye shall hear of wars and rumours of wars: see that ye be not troubled: for all these things must come to pass, but the end is not yet. For nation shall rise against nation, and kingdom against kingdom (Mt 24:6-7).

The four horsemen come with fury and speed, one after the other. As soon as Antichrist arises and reestablishes Temple worship in Jerusalem, a city that three of the world's major religions have a stake in, it will cause destabilization among the Arab nations across the Middle East. And the Antichrist will go forth to *conquer!*

Much discipline is required by the author not to reveal too much too soon. All will be explained in a later chapter on the Antichrist wars. But for now, suffice it to say that we are attempting to give a brief overview of the seals in order to fully explain the difference between the Great Tribulation and the Day of the Lord; that way we can pinpoint the timing of the rapture.

Also, notice Christ's statement in the Olivet Prophecy that *the end is not yet.* At this point of the timeline, we are still in *the beginning of sorrows.*

THE THIRD SEAL –
Famine

And when he had opened the third seal, I heard the third beast say, Come and see. And I beheld, and lo a black horse; and he that sat on him had a pair of balances in his hand. And I heard a voice in the midst of the four beasts say, A measure of wheat for a

penny, and three measures of barley for a penny; and
see thou hurt not the oil and the wine (Rev 6:5-6)

...and there shall be famines, and pestilences... (Mt
24:7).

It's no great stretch to see that wars are usually the
forerunners to famine and disease epidemics.

A pair of scales is used in scripture as a symbol to denote
great famine, as in distributing minute portions of bread to the
hungry (Lev 26:26, Ezek 4:15-16).

And it seems that within the area of this famine, grapes
and olives are preserved, probably for consumption.
Interestingly, *oil and wine* are also figured in the items
Mystery Babylon uses for global trade and commerce later on
during the Great Tribulation (Rev 18:13). So there may be a
deeper meaning there, in that the beast power does not want
to have any scarcity with commodities that are bringing in
fortunes (*hurt not the oil and the wine!*).

THE FOURTH SEAL –
Death

And when he had opened the fourth seal, I heard the
voice of the fourth beast say, Come and see. And I
looked, and behold a pale horse: and his name that
sat on him was Death, and Hell followed with him.
And power was given unto them over the fourth part
of the earth, to kill with sword, and with hunger, and
with death, and with the beasts of the earth (Rev
6:7-8).

This is the only seal in which the horseman is named, and his
name is *Death!* He seems to be a conglomeration of the
previous three seals, but with an acceleration of death as its
main objective. And although a fourth part of the earth is

affected here, that doesn't necessarily mean that a fourth part of humanity is killed off. It's just that many die as a result of wars and famine by Antichrist's claim over this fourth part of the earth.

It's interesting to note, as well, that Antichrist will progressively take more and more control over the earth. At this point of the seals, however, he seems to be only regulating a fourth part of the earth.

It is for this reason that we can be secure in saying that the fourth seal is still not quite the Great Tribulation. For when Antichrist rises to power during the Great Tribulation, he will have obtained a global conquest. We will enlarge upon that point in the chapter devoted to Antichrist's wars.

Another side note to consider is a recent theory regarding the colors of the four horses by those who want to promote a Muslim Antichrist. They conclude that the four colors of the horses are the colors of the Arab flags: white, red, black, green (accepting the fact that *pale* may be translated *green*).

While it's true that many Arab nation flags are composed of those colors, not all are. Iran, Egypt and Saudi Arabia are noticeable among the holdouts. But, as we've noticed "fake news" in the media these days, we also see "fake teachings" among the religious. This is one of them.

Speaking about the Four Horsemen, have you ever wondered why there is an individual horseman for each of the first four seals only, and none thereafter?

WHY ONLY FOUR HORSEMEN?

In ancient times, the best way to announce news or warnings of any sort would be to traverse long distances on horseback. Ancient Rome had what was known as *cursus publicus,* which was the state-run courier and transportation service of the Roman Empire. In early America, we had the Pony Express.

These four horsemen are four separate warnings to the world, each delivering a word of increasing intensity of danger and annihilation! God is pleading with the world during this period of time which Jesus refers to as the *beginning of sorrows* to wake up! These four horsemen are heralding the harrowing time that Jesus calls the *Great Tribulation.* Jesus warns us that it's the worst time of trouble to ever befall the earth, even worse than the time of Noah's flood (Mt 24:21). Keep reading and we'll see that **there will be a way of escape at this time for His people, but it won't be the rapture.**

With each seal becoming more and more intolerable, He is giving ample warning to the world to repent. God demands that we make a choice now about whom we will serve before Satan unleashes his wrath upon the earth in the Fifth Seal. God demands that we make a choice about life or death, righteousness or evil, sonship of God or sonship of Satan, friend of Jesus or friend of the world. Simply put, it's a choice between Jesus or the Antichrist.

So God uses the motif of Four Horsemen as heralds of impending danger in order to emphasize the seriousness of the warning. There's so much we can glean from scripture, even from the slightest details.

Another example of a slight detail that conveys so much is when John is given instructions in heaven by a voice that sounds like a trumpet (Rev 1:10; 4:1). Why does the voice sound like a trumpet? Because, again, it's to denote the urgency of the matter. Trumpets are used to awaken troops, to sound the alarm, and to prepare for war. Therefore the voice sounds like a trumpet so that people can be attentive to the warning! To be forewarned is to be forearmed.

In the days ahead, it will be our closeness to the Lord that is going to keep us protected. Hearing what the Holy Spirit says will guide us into safety and protection. Let's refine our intimacy with Him now and our ability to not only hear the Lord's voice but to follow His directives.

Something else to note about these four horsemen: At no point in God's Word does it say that the work of these horsemen is *God's wrath upon mankind.*

The scriptures are very transparent when it comes to God's wrath upon mankind. The Word will tell us when it's God's wrath. These four horsemen ride at the time that coincides with the *rise* of Antichrist, who is pushing his satanic system upon the whole world. We haven't come to the Great Tribulation yet. And we haven't come to the Day of the Lord yet. Up till now, we've only covered the first three and a half years of Daniel's seven year prophecy. But, in the next chapter, as we pass through the midpoint of Daniel's seven year period, we will finally begin to see the distinct difference between the Great Tribulation and the Day of the Lord, and we'll be able to know the exact *watch of the night* and the exact *times and seasons* for Christ's return and the rapture.

6
GREAT TRIBULATION IS NOT GOD'S WRATH

They say the Great Tribulation is the wrath of God. They combine the Great Tribulation and the Day of the Lord into *one* event. They say the rapture takes place *before* the Great Tribulation. They say a loving Father would never allow His children to be on the earth during Antichrist's reign. They twist scriptures that are on a predetermined chronological timeline to suit their own needs, to make the scriptures say what they want them to say.

As we've said, so much confusion!

In this chapter, let's debunk it all and bring clarity and truth to the table. This chapter is for the remnant, for those who eagerly desire the truth of the Bible and will receive and believe His Word. It's time we unpack the most misunderstood part of eschatology – the difference between the Great Tribulation and the Day of the Lord, and the difference between Satan's wrath (through tribulation) and God's wrath.

We can all agree that God *has* promised His people that they will not be partakers of His wrath. Scripture lays that promise out:

*Much more then, being now justified by his blood, **we shall be saved from wrath through him*** (Rom 5:9)

*And to wait for his Son from heaven, whom he raised from the dead, even **Jesus, which delivered us from the wrath to come*** (1Thess 1:10)

***For God hath not appointed us to wrath,** but to obtain salvation by our Lord Jesus Christ* (1Thess 5:9).

His wrath is reserved for the children of disobedience.

*He that believeth on the Son hath everlasting life: and **he that believeth not the Son shall not see life; but the wrath of God abideth on him*** (Jn 3:36)

For the wrath of God is revealed from heaven against all ungodliness and unrighteousness of men, who hold the truth in unrighteousness (Rom 1:18)

*For which things' sake **the wrath of God cometh on the children of disobedience*** (Col 3:6).

So we're all in agreement at this point. Yet, conversely, the scriptures never describe *tribulation* as part of God's wrath. Please understand that. In fact, how often in scripture does it promise that tribulation will come upon the children of God?

*These things I have spoken unto you, that in me ye might have peace. **In the world ye shall have tribulation: but be of good cheer; I have overcome the world*** (Jn 16:33)

*Confirming the souls of the disciples, and exhorting them to continue in the faith, and that **we must through much tribulation enter into the kingdom of God*** (Acts 14:22)

> ***Who comforteth us in all our tribulation,*** *that we may be able to comfort them which are in any trouble, by the comfort wherewith we ourselves are comforted of God* (2 Cor 1:4)

> Jesus tells the church of Smyrna: ***I know thy works, and tribulation...*** (Rev 2:2)

> ***Who shall separate us from the love of Christ? shall tribulation, or distress, or persecution, or famine, or nakedness, or peril, or sword?*** (Rom 8:35).

The last scripture, of course, speaks to those who feel that a loving God could never allow His children to go through tough times, much less the Great Tribulation. Yet in all this, God's love is not extinguished, nor are His plans and purposes for us annulled, nor is our eternal future in jeopardy.

Having said all that, God has promised to protect a segment of His people during the Great Tribulation. Some will indeed give glory to God by giving up their lives in martyrdom like the great saints of old and like those in the Middle East today. And on the other hand, some will indeed give glory to God by being protected from Tribulation (i.e., being *accounted worthy to escape* the wrath of Satan) until His return. More about that later on in the book.

Now let's get on with the crux of the issue. God has left an indelibly written retort to those who believe the Great Tribulation is the same as the Day of the Lord. Once you understand this next portion of scripture, you cannot legitimately argue that they are one event and you cannot arbitrarily select a convenient time for your rapture. **God's timeline for the rapture is confirmed by the next three seals.**

THE FIFTH SEAL –
The Great Tribulation

And when he had opened the fifth seal, I saw under the altar the souls of them that were slain for the word of God, and for the testimony which they held: and they cried with a loud voice, saying, How long, O Lord, holy and true, dost thou not judge and avenge our blood on them that dwell on the earth. And white robes were given unto them, that they should rest yet for a little season, until their fellowservants also and their brethren, that should be killed as they were, should be fulfilled (Rev 6:9).

There are many ways for God to have described this seal. He could have highlighted the fact that Satan has empowered the Antichrist and the False Prophet to bring the world to its knees in a helpless global display of servitude, worship, and bondage. God could have described this time, as Christ had elsewhere (Mt 24:21), as the worst time of trouble the world will ever know or experience. And, if He didn't intervene, there would be no more life left on earth (Mt 24:22).

Instead, God poignantly describes the horror that His children face at this time in a symbolic dialogue between His children and Himself . His whole attention is wrapped around His children who are seeking retribution upon those Antichrist forces on the earth. (*And shall He not avenge His own elect which cry day and night to Him...?* Lk 18:7).

Here is the martyrdom of the saints, which Christ forewarned us about in Matthew 24:9: *then shall they deliver you up to be afflicted and shall kill you. And you shall be hated of all nations for My name's sake.*

As an aside, many pre-tribulationists will insist that Matthew 24 is referring to Jews being hated and killed, and that this section in Matthew, in general, is speaking to the Jews and warning *them.* Well, how many Jews are persecuted and killed for *His name's sake?* Only Christians are persecuted for *His* name's sake – the precious name of Jesus, that is above all other names and for whom Christians are so aptly named.

Simply, **the Great Tribulation is Satan's wrath against God's people.** This is one of those important insights to keep in mind in order to properly understand prophecy.

> *And when the dragon saw that he was cast unto the earth, he persecuted the woman which brought forth the man child... **And the dragon was wroth with the woman, and went to make war with the remnant of her seed, which keep the commandments of God, and have the testimony of Jesus Christ** (Rev 12:13, 17).*

So we have seen how the previous seals chronologically lead up to the Great Tribulation. The first four seals, the Four Horsemen, warn the world about this fifth seal. You will now see how the next two seals – that come *after* the Great Tribulation – become so pivotal in understanding the timing of the Rapture.

THE SIXTH SEAL –
Signs in the Sun, Moon and Stars

> *And I beheld when he had opened the sixth seal, and, lo, there was a great earthquake; and the sun became black as sackcloth of hair, and the moon became as blood; and the stars of heaven fell unto the earth, even as a fig tree casteth her untimely figs, when she is shaken of a mighty wind (Rev 6:12-13).*

Remember, Jesus said, *Immediately **after the tribulation** of those days shall the sun be darkened, and the moon shall not give her light,* *and the stars shall fall from heaven, and the powers of the heavens shall be shaken* (Mt 24:29)?

Yes, *after* the tribulation comes this phenomenal sign of the darkening of the universe, preparing the heavenly stage for the return of Jesus Christ. This is the supernatural warning that God is wresting control of the earth from the spiritual powers that be.

Talk about making a grand entrance. No one has created or imagined a more spectacularly creative entrance than this. And, this cannot be attributed to a solar eclipse, as some have falsely claimed in the past.

The sun literally goes dark, getting the whole world's attention. The moon turns bloody red. No one can escape this unprecedented heavenly phenomenon. The stars of the universe fall. Darkness is upon the earth. The next seal, as we shall see, is the return of Jesus Christ, who alone deserves the honor of the supernatural dimming of all natural lights and their bowing down, metaphorically, to the Creator of all as He breaks through the gross darkness with the brightness of His glory just as lightning that illuminates the sky from one end of heaven to the other (Mt 24:27)!

How remarkably majestic!

God is now putting the world on notice that He is intervening to stop Antichrist's reign and desolation of his own making.

But we're getting ahead of ourselves. Suffice it to say, **the sixth seal separates the Great Tribulation from the next seal, the Day of the Lord.**

This is another important insight. There can be no misunderstanding. There is no room for confusion. Pre-tribulationists never talk about the sixth seal because it doesn't fit in with their theology. The sixth seal forcefully and dramatically separates the Great Tribulation from the Day of the Lord.

THE GREAT TRIBULATION IS NOT THE DAY OF THE LORD

What this sixth seal does is prove that the **Great Tribulation** is *not at all* a part of the **Day of the Lord** – that the two events are totally *opposite* in purpose and are totally separated by this supernatural event. Many people misread prophetic scriptures because they don't know when one begins and the other ends. Therefore they read scriptures meant for the Day of the Lord as if it was in the Great Tribulation, and vice versa.

Let's go again to Christ's comments on the Mount of Olives:

> *Immediately after the tribulation of those days shall the sun be darkened, and the moon shall not give her light, and the stars shall fall from heaven, and the powers of the heavens shall be shaken* (Mt 24:29).

When Jesus says, *immediately after the tribulation*, He is carefully following the chronological pattern outlined in Revelation. And once this sixth seal occurs, the tribulation is over – and the Day of the Lord will soon begin!

Old Testament prophets, including Isaiah, knew well that the signs in the sun, moon and stars were the warning signs of the Lord's wrath on the Day of the Lord.

> ***Howl ye; for the day of the LORD is at hand;*** *it shall come as a destruction from the Almighty. Therefore shall all hands be faint, and every man's heart shall melt: And they shall be afraid: pangs and sorrows shall take hold of them; they shall be in pain as a woman that travaileth: they shall be amazed one at another; their faces shall be as flames.* ***Behold, the day of the LORD cometh, cruel***

both with wrath and fierce anger, to lay the land desolate: and he shall destroy the sinners thereof out of it. For the stars of heaven and the constellations thereof shall not give their light: the sun shall be darkened in his going forth, and the moon shall not cause her light to shine. And I will punish the world for their evil, and the wicked for their iniquity; and I will cause the arrogancy of the proud to cease, and will lay low the haughtiness of the terrible (Isa 13:6-11).

Joel also confirms Revelation, giving more precise details about the Day of the Lord. The whole theme of his book can be summed up in this one scripture:

Alas for the Day of the Lord is at hand (Joel 1:15).

He, too, confirms that signs in the heavens signals the beginning of the Day of the Lord.

*The sun shall be turned into darkness, and the moon into blood, **before the great and the terrible day of the LORD come*** (Joel 2:31).

The Great Tribulation is *not* the terrible Day of the Lord! The Great Tribulation is not God's judgment, nor is it His wrath.

But while we're in the book of Joel, let's backtrack for a little tangent just to encourage the Body of believers. God promises that He will pour out His Spirit upon the world just *before* the Day of the Lord!

And it shall come to pass afterward, that I will pour out my spirit upon all flesh; and your sons and your daughters shall prophesy, your old men shall dream dreams, your young men shall see visions (Joel 2:28).

You may shudder thinking about the end times, wondering how one could possibly endure such hostility, wretchedness and persecution in the world. But remember that God will be pouring out His Spirit in an unprecedented way. How do you think that we could endure the horrific last days except God be in us with might? Expect that God will invigorate us with supernatural powers, empower us with immutable, jewel-refined faith, and enrich us with hope and determination that repels the satanic horrors in the world. When He says He's going to pour out His Spirit, get ready for a blast of the Holy Ghost that's LIFE-sustaining against the onslaught of the enemy – POWER you've never seen before!

> *And it shall come to pass, that whosoever shall call*
> *on the name of the Lord shall be delivered, as*
> *the Lord hath said, and in the remnant whom the*
> *Lord shall call* (Joel 2:32).

At a time when pre-tribulationists want to escape the Great Tribulation in a rapture, God desires to have His children harvesting the world. And He will empower, equip and protect us as we do this work.

Again, for review – for there is nothing quite like reviewing new truth to dispense of old mindsets – Christ said that the supernatural signs in the heavens will happen immediately *after the Great Tribulation*, and Joel tells us that these same supernatural signs in the heavens happen *before the Day of the Lord*. Therefore these two events cannot be the same thing!

Now we have understanding: **the sixth seal's heavenly signs are a dividing line between the Great Tribulation and the Day of the Lord.** Let there be no more confusion of this matter again. And the rapture, as we will soon see, will correspond with the Day of the Lord!

DAY OF THE LORD IS GOD'S WRATH

We've already seen that the Great Tribulation is *Satan's* wrath against God's people. Now let's take a look at other scriptures describing the Day of the Lord as *God's* wrath.

> *Alas for the day! For the Day of the Lord is at hand, and as a destruction from the Almighty shall it come* (Joel 1:15).

Continue now in Revelation 6, where the end times are laid out in chronological order. Following the sixth seal of the heavenly signs, we read of fearful humanity expecting divine judgment from God in the soon-coming seventh seal.

> *And the kings of the earth, the great men, the rich men, the commanders, the mighty men, every slave and every free man, hid themselves in the caves and in the rocks of the mountains, and said to the mountains and rocks, "Fall on us and **hide us from the face of Him who sits on the throne and from the wrath of the Lamb! For the great day of His wrath has come, and who is able to stand?"**** (Rev 6:15-17).

But where is the Lord's wrath directed? Isaiah continues this same train of thought as Revelation:

> *Enter into the rock, and hide in the dust, From the terror of the LORD And the glory of His majesty. The lofty looks of man shall be humbled, The haughtiness of men shall be bowed down, And the LORD alone shall be exalted in that day. For the day of the LORD of hosts shall come upon everything proud and lofty, Upon everything lifted up—And it shall be brought low—Upon all the cedars of Lebanon that are high and lifted up, And upon all the oaks of Bashan; Upon all the high mountains, And upon all the hills that are*

lifted up; Upon every high tower, And upon every fortified wall; Upon all the ships of Tarshish, And upon all the beautiful sloops. The loftiness of man shall be bowed down, And the haughtiness of men shall be brought low; The LORD alone will be exalted in that day, But the idols He shall utterly abolish. **They shall go into the holes of the rocks, And into the caves of the earth, From the terror of the LORD And the glory of His majesty, When He arises to shake the earth mightily. In that day a man will cast away his idols of silver And his idols of gold, Which they made, each for himself to worship, To the moles and bats, To go into the clefts of the rocks, And into the crags of the rugged rocks, From the terror of the LORD And the glory of His majesty, When He arises to shake the earth mightily** (Isa 2:10-21).

This is talking about the Lord's wrath against the wicked! And wherever you see in scripture: *the day; the Day of the Lord; the wrath; the day of His wrath; the end; the end of the age* – it is always talking about the Day of the Lord, *not* the Great Tribulation.

Behold, the day of the LORD comes, Cruel, with both wrath and fierce anger, To lay the land desolate; And He will destroy its sinners from it. **For the stars of heaven and their constellations Will not give their light; The sun will be darkened in its going forth, And the moon will not cause its light to shine. I will punish the world for its evil,** *And the wicked for their iniquity; I will halt the arrogance of the proud, And will lay low the haughtiness of the terrible* (Isa 13:9-11)

For behold, the day is coming, Burning like an oven, And all the proud, yes, all who do wickedly will be stubble. And the day which is coming shall burn them up, Says the LORD of hosts, That will leave them neither root nor branch (Mal 4:1).

Neither shall the rich men escape, who, behind the scenes in order to gain more power and wealth, greedily cause havoc and ruination in all the nations and push a satanic control upon the people. Whether they be called Illuminati, Deep State, Shadow Government, the Rothschilds, Council of Foreign Relations, Bilderberg group, Federal Reserve, or whatever, even they shall not be overlooked by the Judge of all the earth. Retribution is finally meted out on them who pull the world's strings:

> *Go to now, ye rich men, weep and howl for your miseries that shall come upon you. Your riches are corrupted, and your garments are moth eaten. Your gold and silver is cankered; and the rust of them shall be a witness against you, and shall eat your flesh as it were fire. Ye have heaped treasure together for the last days. Behold, the hire of the labourers who have reaped down your fields, which is of you kept back by fraud, crieth: and the cries of them which have reaped are entered into the ears of the Lord of sabaoth. Ye have lived in pleasure on the earth, and been wanton; ye have nourished your hearts, as in a day of slaughter. Ye have condemned and killed the just; and he doth not resist you. Be patient therefore, brethren, unto the coming of the Lord* (Jas 5:1-7).

But we still haven't pinpointed the timing of the rapture. Hold on. We're getting to it. We're almost there.

THE SEVENTH SEAL –
The Day of the Lord

Even though we've practically defined the Day of the Lord already, we still need to wrap up what Revelation says about this seventh seal. Once the wicked see the signs in the heavens, they cry out from their hiding places:

And said to the mountains and rocks, Fall on us, and hide us from the face of him that sitteth on the throne, and from the wrath of the Lamb: For the great day of his wrath is come; and who shall be able to stand? (Rev 6:16-17).

And, sure enough, the next seal describes the judgment plagues that will be poured out upon the unrepentant wicked. So horrific and so consequential is this next seal upon the eternal destinies of so many on the earth that heaven interrupts its regular joyful sounds of worship in order to silently mourn these self-aborted children.

And when he had opened the seventh seal, there was silence in heaven about the space of half an hour (Rev 8:1).

Can you imagine the tears and sorrow that heaven experiences here? There are some things that bring such deep pain to God in ways that we may never fully understand nor appreciate. Something is going to happen now that is so striking, so cataclysmic that Heaven itself is silenced!

And I saw the seven angels which stood before God; and to them were given seven trumpets (Rev 8:2).

If you read through this portion of scripture and subsequent chapters, you'll find that these angels are each given trumpets, and when they blast their trumpets, judgments are being poured out upon the wicked as upon the earth: (vs 6) *hail and fire*; (vs 8) *a third of the sea turned into blood*; etc.

It finally culminates with the seventh trumpet. In the same way that the seventh seal is comprised of the seven trumpet judgments (Rev 8, 9, 11:15-18), the seventh trumpet judgment is comprised of the seven last plagues (Rev 15, 16), which *completes* the Wrath of God (Rev 15:1). The term Armageddon can be safely placed within the timeframe of the Day of the Lord.

Something else to consider about the Day of the Lord is that it's *not* a day in length. The term *day* signifies a period of time. For instance, the judgment of the fifth trumpet angel is five months of torment (Rev 9:5, 10). It's possible that the Day of the Lord lasts up to a year.

There's more to be learned from the book of Revelation. We're sure that as the days move perilously close to the Great Tribulation, the Holy Spirit will impart greater understanding on all aspects of this book and the rest of the Bible.

While it's not within the scope of this book to discuss all particulars of the Day of the Lord, it is our intention to show a correlation between the seven seals of Revelation and the Olivet Prophecy, and how it all ties in to Daniel's seven years. We've shown that Jesus is the Revealer of the seals and that there is a definite timeline of chronological events in the last days which cannot be broken. We have proven that there is a definite distinction between the Great Tribulation and the Day of the Lord. All this was necessary to explain that there is no possibility of a pre-tribulation rapture.

Thankfully you've been following along up till now. So let's finally see what Christ says about the timing of the rapture in the Olivet Prophecy.

THE RAPTURE PINPOINTED

Immediately after the tribulation of those days the sun will be darkened, and the moon will not give its light; the stars will fall from heaven, and the powers of the heavens will be shaken. Then the sign of the Son of Man will appear in heaven, and then all the tribes of the earth will mourn, and they will see the Son of Man coming on the clouds of heaven with power and great glory. And He will send His angels with a great sound

of a trumpet, and they will gather together His elect
from the four winds, from one end of heaven to the
other (Mt 24:29-31).

It really can't be plainer than this. Jesus lays out the
chronological order of events before His return: tribulation;
signs in the sun, moon and stars; the sign of the Son of Man
in heaven returning to earth (i.e., the *Parousia*, that radiant
display of Christ's glory bursting the darkness and seen from
one end of the earth to the other); the wicked mourn their
doom; Christ receives His elect from the four winds of
heaven, as they have been resurrected worldwide from their
immediate locations on the globe.

Clear and simple. Now, as we've seen, both the Olivet
Prophecy and Revelation go hand in hand. If this is where
Jesus is pinpointing the rapture, then the book of Revelation
ought to confirm this too. And, it *does!*

Keep in mind that Revelation lays out the end times in
chronologic fashion. We've seen Revelation 6 detail and
explain the six seals opened up by Jesus and how this was all
corroborated by Jesus' Olivet Prophecy. Now before Jesus
opens up the seventh seal in Revelation 8, which is the Day
of God's wrath and judgment, there is an inset chapter in
Revelation 7 explaining what is going on between the sixth
and seventh seals.

Let's review chapter seven together. The first three
verses show God forestalling the angels of judgment from
carrying out their destruction upon the earth. This chapter will
later show the rapture of the saints. But before that, we see
God marking out 144,000 people with a seal.

And after these things I saw four angels standing on
the four corners of the earth, holding the four winds
of the earth, that the wind should not blow on the
earth, nor on the sea, nor on any tree. And I saw
another angel ascending from the east, having the
seal of the living God: and he cried with a loud voice

*to the four angels, to whom it was given to hurt the earth and the sea, **Saying, Hurt not the earth, neither the sea, nor the trees, till we have sealed the servants of our God in their foreheads. And I heard the number of them which were sealed: and there were sealed an hundred and forty and four thousand of all the tribes of the children of Israel.***

Judah	*= 12,000*
Reuben	*= 12,000*
Gad	*= 12,000*
Aser	*= 12,000*
Nephtalim	*= 12,000*
Manasseh	*= 12,000*
Simeon	*= 12,000*
Levi	*=12,000*
Issachar	*= 12,000*
Zabulon	*= 12,000*
Joseph	*= 12,000*
Benjamin	*= 12,000*

(Rev 7:1-8).

Many mistakenly speculate that this is the Church – it's not! Nor does God mark these individuals for the purpose of proclaiming the gospel. They don't. Please notice that the text does not say anything about them *spreading the gospel.* They are *not* spreading the gospel because judgment is now upon the world and there's no more room for repentance. Yet if we're willing to accept the Word at face value, the scriptures explain that God seals them because they are 12,000 representatives from each of the 12 tribes of Israel, including the lost tribes, amassing to 144,000.

This is not a spiritual seal for a spiritual people. This is a protective seal that insolates a physical remnant of Israel to live through the Day of the Lord, the purpose of which shall be made more plain as we continue.

Ezekiel explains further in a companion chapter to Revelation 7. Here, too, Ezekiel describes a heavenly meeting in which destroying angels are told to hold off until certain Israelites are marked for protection against the approaching wrath of God (Ezek 8:18-9:1-3).

> *And the LORD said unto him, Go through the midst of the city, through the midst of Jerusalem, and **set a mark upon the foreheads of the men that sigh and that cry for all the abominations that be done in the midst thereof.** And to the others he said in mine hearing, Go ye after him through the city, and smite: let not your eye spare, neither have ye pity: Slay utterly old and young, both maids, and little children, and women: **but come not near any man upon whom is the mark;** and begin at my sanctuary. Then they began at the ancient men which were before the house...And, behold, the man clothed with linen, which had the inkhorn by his side, reported the matter, saying, I have done as thou hast commanded me* (Ezek 9:4-6, 11).

God chooses to protect them in part because of their concern and sorrow *for all the abominations that be done* in Jerusalem.

Going back to Revelation we see more developments in the lives of the 144,000. Both Revelation 7 and Ezekiel 9 picture the 144,000 being *sealed* or *marked*, which in this case are synonymous terms. The timeframes for both are also just *before* the return of the Lord, and specifically just before the destruction of Jerusalem (Ezek 9:4, Rev 18:4).

We need to elaborate on Revelation 18:4 and understand the timeframe it's picturing:

> *And I heard another voice from heaven, saying, **Come out of her, my people, that ye be not partakers of her sins, and that ye receive not of her plagues*** (Rev 18:4).

This entire chapter deals with the destruction of Mystery Babylon, which we will explore in a later chapter. The timeframe is during the Day of the Lord, which is months long. We will soon see the saints of God are already raptured by this point, so it can't be referring to them. Who then could this group be? It can only be referring to the 144,000 physical Israelites, who lived through the ravages of the Day of the Lord, have become acquainted with the Lord Jesus during that time, and are now glorified right after the total destruction of Jerusalem.

Once the Lord is situated on Mount Zion, we see in Revelation 14 that the 144,000 are with Him!

> *And I looked, and, lo, a Lamb stood on the mount Sion, and with him an hundred forty and four thousand, having his Father's name written in their foreheads* (Rev 14:1).

Suddenly the 144,000 are united with the returned Lord in Mount Zion, which symbolizes the region from which the New Jerusalem will be centered. They are sealed with the name of the Father upon their foreheads. In a remarkable contrast between the mark of the beast and God's seal, we see that when God puts a seal on someone, they are protected and given eternal life. It's important to note that they started out as a physical people protected during the Day of the Lord and now they are saved and with the Lord after He returns.

The Word calls them the *redeemed from the earth* (vs 3) and the *firstfruits unto God and to the Lamb* (vs 4).

That's an interesting phrase. Why are they called the *firstfruits unto God and to the Lamb?*

Our Savior is wasting no time in setting the stage for saving the world *throughout* the New Millennium. These are the firstfruits of humans who ascend to sonship status, whose corruptible bodies are changed to become incorruptible and eternal. These are transfigured children of God, examples for generations upon generations to follow.

This is why angels go forth to proclaim the gospel throughout the traumatized earth in Revelation 14:5-6. The "New World Order" has finally arrived, but it's the Lord's New World Order. New management has arrived.

The sealing of the 144,000 is fulfillment, if not totally at least in part, that "all Israel will be saved." And it's also wonderfully illustrative of a loving God offering eternal life to everyone on the earth from henceforth, even forever.

The people on the earth will still have to fight their own stubborn flesh, as Zechariah points out:

> *And it shall come to pass, that every one that is left of all the nations which came against Jerusalem shall even go up from year to year to worship the King, the LORD of hosts, and to keep the feast of tabernacles. And it shall be, that whoso will not come up of all the families of the earth unto Jerusalem to worship the King, the LORD of hosts, even upon them shall be no rain. And if the family of Egypt go not up, and come not, that have no rain; there shall be the plague, wherewith the LORD will smite the heathen that come not up to keep the feast of tabernacles. This shall be the punishment of Egypt, and the punishment of all nations that come not up to keep the feast of tabernacles* (Zech 14:16-19).

But let's get back to the most important part – the rapture of the Saints. As we continue in Revelation 7, we see a second group of people:

> **After this I beheld, and, lo, a great multitude, which no man could number, of all nations, and kindreds, and people, and tongues, stood before the throne, and before the Lamb, clothed with white robes, and palms in their hands; And cried with a loud voice,**

saying, Salvation to our God which sitteth upon the throne, and unto the Lamb. And all the angels stood round about the throne, and about the elders and the four beasts, and fell before the throne on their faces, and worshipped God, Saying, Amen: Blessing, and glory, and wisdom, and thanksgiving, and honour, and power, and might, be unto our God for ever and ever. Amen. And one of the elders answered, saying unto me, What are these which are arrayed in white robes? and whence came they? And I said unto him, Sir, thou knowest. And he said to me, These are they which came out of great tribulation, and have washed their robes, and made them white in the blood of the Lamb. Therefore are they before the throne of God, and serve him day and night in his temple: and he that sitteth on the throne shall dwell among them. They shall hunger no more, neither thirst any more; neither shall the sun light on them, nor any heat. For the Lamb which is in the midst of the throne shall feed them, and shall lead them unto living fountains of waters: and God shall wipe away all tears from their eyes (Rev 7:9-17).

How did this innumerable multitude, redeemed among men, appear at God's throne? The rapture has just occurred! God has both sealed physical Israel on the earth and has raptured spiritual Israel, including dead saints, into His presence just before He metes out judgment upon the earth.

Let's review now and see other scriptures come to life with this new understanding.

RAPTURE & WRATH OF GOD TOGETHER IN SCRIPTURE

Concerning the coming of our Lord Jesus Christ and our being gathered to Him... (2 Thess 2:1).

Stop right there. Here the Apostle Paul equates as a united event the coming of Jesus Christ and our being gathered together to Him. The only time Christ makes His appearance is in the Day of the Lord.

> *Concerning the coming of our Lord Jesus Christ and our being gathered to Him, we ask you, Brothers, not to become easily unsettled or alarmed by some prophecy, report or letter supposed to have come from us, saying* **the Day of the Lord has already come** *(2 Thess 2:1-2).*

Again, Paul asserts that the coming of the Lord with our being gathered to Him *pertains* to the Day of the Lord.

And he *forewarns* God's people not to fall for any other doctrine that misrepresents the timing of the rapture – even though it comes from legitimate sources, whether prophecies or apostolic decrees. This warning refers also to those who think that all prophecies were fulfilled in 70 AD.

> *Don't let anyone deceive you in any way, for that day* (the Day of the Lord and the rapture of the saints) *will not come until the rebellion occurs and the man of lawlessness is revealed, the man doomed to destruction. He will oppose and will exalt himself over everything that is called God or is worshipped, so that he sets himself up in God's temple, proclaiming himself to be God* (2 Thess 2:3-4).

Paul is saying exactly what we've been teaching. The Church will be present on the earth as Antichrist not only rises to power but sets himself up as god in the newly erected Temple in Jerusalem! We will be here on earth to see this with our own eyes as it's broadcast over television and Internet. He will demand worship from all in the world during the Great Tribulation or they will be harassed and persecuted. And, Paul says, we are on the earth at that time.

Let that sink in.

Yet as we've already seen earlier in this chapter, the Church is protected from his wrath. And we're protected because Jesus takes us out of the world so that He can pour out His wrath on the earth.

> *He is ready to separate the chaff from the wheat with his winnowing fork. Then he will clean up the threshing area,* **gathering the wheat into his barn but burning the chaff with never-ending fire**
> (Lk 3:17, NLT).

Jesus gives us the parable of the wheat and the tares.

> *Another parable put he forth unto them, saying, The kingdom of heaven is likened unto a man which sowed good seed in his field: But while men slept, his enemy came and sowed tares among the wheat, and went his way. But when the blade was sprung up, and brought forth fruit, then appeared the tares also. So the servants of the householder came and said unto him, Sir, didst not thou sow good seed in thy field? from whence then hath it tares? He said unto them, An enemy hath done this. The servants said unto him, Wilt thou then that we go and gather them up? But he said, Nay; lest while ye gather up the tares, ye root up also the wheat with them. Let both grow together until the harvest: and* **in the time of harvest I will say to the reapers, Gather ye together first the tares, and bind them in bundles to burn them: but gather the wheat into my barn** (Mt 13:24-30).

The story of Noah affirms God's method of removing His people from impending disaster. As soon as Noah's family was well protected in the ark, judgment came upon the world in that week (Gen 7:7-10).

The story of Lot again shows us God removing His people before swift judgment comes upon the land (Gen 19).

And as it was in the days of Noe, so shall it be also in the days of the Son of man. They did eat, they drank, they married wives, they were given in marriage, until the day that Noe entered into the ark, and the flood came, and destroyed them all. Likewise also as it was in the days of Lot; they did eat, they drank, they bought, they sold, they planted, they builded; But the same day that Lot went out of Sodom it rained fire and brimstone from heaven, and destroyed them all. Even thus shall it be in the day when the Son of man is revealed. In that day, he which shall be upon the housetop, and his stuff in the house, let him not come down to take it away: and he that is in the field, let him likewise not return back. Remember Lot's wife. Whosoever shall seek to save his life shall lose it; and whosoever shall lose his life shall preserve it. I tell you, in that night there shall be two men in one bed; the one shall be taken, and the other shall be left. Two women shall be grinding together; the one shall be taken, and the other left. Two men shall be in the field; the one shall be taken, and the other left. And they answered and said unto him, Where, Lord? And he said unto them, Wheresoever the body is, thither will the eagles be gathered together (Lk 17:26-37).

And the eagles are gathered together with the Body (the Lord) on the Day of the Lord. Therefore, God *does* promise us that He will remove us before *His wrath* and judgment (Rom 5:9, I Thess 1:10, 5:9), but His wrath is referring to the Day of the Lord and *not* the Great Tribulation.

> *That the wicked is reserved to the day of destruction?* **they shall be brought forth to the day of wrath** (Job 21:30)

> *Behold,* **the day of the LORD cometh, cruel both with wrath and fierce anger**, *to lay the land desolate: and he shall destroy the sinners thereof out of it...*

*Therefore I will shake the heavens, and the earth shall remove out of her place, **in the wrath of the LORD of hosts, and in the day of his fierce anger*** (Isa 13:9, 13)

*The time is come, **the day draweth near**: let not the buyer rejoice, nor the seller mourn: **for wrath is upon all the multitude thereof**... They shall cast their silver in the streets, and their gold shall be removed: their silver and their gold shall not be able to deliver them in **the day of the wrath of the LORD**: they shall not satisfy their souls, neither fill their bowels: because it is the stumbling block of their iniquity* (Ezek 7:12, 19)

***For in my jealousy and in the fire of my wrath** have I spoken, Surely **in that day** there shall be a great shaking in the land of Israel* (Ezek 38:19)

***That day is a day of wrath, a day of trouble and distress, a day of wasteness and desolation, a day of darkness and gloominess, a day of clouds and thick darkness**... Neither their silver nor their gold shall be able to deliver them in **the day of the LORD'S wrath;** but the whole land shall be devoured by the fire of his jealousy: for he shall make even a speedy riddance of all them that dwell in the land* (Zeph 1:15, 18)

*But after thy hardness and impenitent heart treasurest up unto thyself wrath against **the day of wrath and revelation of the righteous judgment of God*** (Rom 2:5)

***For the great day of his wrath is come;** and who shall be able to stand?* (Rev 6:17).

NOT ONLY SAVED FROM WRATH, BUT GLORIFIED!

*So also is the resurrection of the dead. **It is sown in***

corruption; it is raised in incorruption: It is sown in dishonour; it is raised in glory: it is sown in weakness; it is raised in power: It is sown a natural body; it is raised a spiritual body. *There is a natural body, and there is a spiritual body...Now this I say, brethren, that flesh and blood cannot inherit the kingdom of God; neither doth corruption inherit incorruption. Behold, I shew you a mystery; We shall not all sleep, but we shall all be changed,* **In a moment, in the twinkling of an eye, at the last trump: for the trumpet shall sound, and the dead shall be raised incorruptible, and we shall be changed. For this corruptible must put on incorruption, and this mortal must put on immortality. So when this corruptible shall have put on incorruption, and this mortal shall have put on immortality,** *then shall be brought to pass the saying that is written, Death is swallowed up in victory. O death, where is thy sting? O grave, where is thy victory? ... But thanks be to God, which giveth us the victory through our Lord Jesus Christ* (1Cor 15:42-44, 50-55, 57)

But if the Spirit of him that raised up Jesus from the dead dwell in you, he that raised up Christ from the dead shall also **quicken your mortal bodies** *by his Spirit that dwelleth in you... The Spirit itself beareth witness with our spirit, that we are the children of God: And if children, then heirs; heirs of God, and joint-heirs with Christ; if so be that we suffer with him, that* **we may be also glorified together.** *For I reckon that the sufferings of this present time are not worthy to be compared with* **the glory which shall be revealed in us.** *For the earnest expectation of the creature waiteth for the manifestation of the sons of God... For we know that the whole creation groaneth and travaileth in pain together until now. And not only they, but ourselves also, which have the firstfruits of the Spirit, even we ourselves groan*

*within ourselves, waiting for the adoption, to wit, **the redemption of our body*** (Rom 8:11, 16-19, 22-23)
*For our conversation is in heaven; from whence also we look for the Saviour, **the Lord Jesus Christ: Who shall change our vile body, that it may be fashioned like unto his glorious body**, according to the working whereby he is able even to subdue all things unto himself* (Phil 3:20-21)

*Dear friends, now we are children of God, and what we will be has not yet been made known. But we know that **when he appears, we shall be like him**, for we shall see him as he is* (1 Jn 3:2).

SECRET RAPTURE NOT SO SECRET

Those who would support a secret rapture before Christ's actual coming in glory must realize that there is no scriptural support for a secret rapture.

*For **the Son of Man in His day** (the Day of the Lord) **will be like lightning**, which flashes and lights up the sky from one end to the other* (Lk 17:24)

*And when he had spoken these things, while they beheld, he was taken up; and a cloud received him out of their sight. And while they looked stedfastly toward heaven as he went up, behold, two men stood by them in white apparel; Which also said, Ye men of Galilee, why stand ye gazing up into heaven? **this same Jesus, which is taken up from you into heaven, shall so come in like manner as ye have seen him go into heaven*** (Acts 1:9-11)

*Behold, He is coming with clouds, **and every eye will see Him*** (Rev 1:7)

*For the **Lord Himself will come down from Heaven, with a loud command, with the voice of the*** *archangel and with the trumpet call of God, and the dead in Christ will rise first. After that, we who are still alive and are left will be caught up together with them in the clouds to meet the Lord in the air. And so we will be with the Lord forever. Therefore encourage each other with these words* (1 Thess 4:16-18)

*They will see the Son of Man coming on the clouds of heaven with power and great glory. And **He will send His angels with a great sound of a trumpet**, and they will gather together His elect from the four winds, from one end of heaven to the other* (Mt 24:30-31).

SYMMETRY OF GOD'S WORD

We've seen how that many teach amiss the timing of the rapture because of a total inability to discern the difference between the Great Tribulation and the Day of the Lord, among other things. They say the Great Tribulation is seven years; scripture says that it is three and a half years.

Understanding this fact allows all the pieces of bible prophesy to fall into place. With this in mind, we can see related scriptures and how they line up nicely with this truth.

• Antichrist's reign is 3 ½ years
Daniel already told us that Antichrist's reign is three and a half years, from the time he enters the Temple as god till the consummation of all things (Christ's return). Revelation confirms this:

*The beast (Antichrist) was given a mouth speaking proud words and blasphemies, **and he was permitted to exercise ruling authority for forty-two months** *(Rev 13:5).

• Persecution of the saints lasts 3 ½ years
Jesus tells His followers to flee from persecution (Mt 24:16). Some will be persecuted, others will flee. Some will give

glory to God by giving up their lives. Some will give glory to God by being protected during this time and remain alive at His return.

.

> *But the woman was given the two wings of a giant eagle so that **she could fly out into the wilderness, to the place God prepared for her, where she is taken care of — away from the presence of the serpent — for a time, times, and half a time** (Rev 12:14, NET).*

• **The Two Witnesses prophesy for 3 ½ years**
> ***And I will grant my two witnesses authority to prophesy for 1,260 days,*** *dressed in sackcloth. (These are the two olive trees and the two lampstands that stand before the Lord of the earth.) If anyone wants to harm them, fire comes out of their mouths and completely consumes their enemies. If anyone wants to harm them, they must be killed this way (Rev 11:3-5, NET).*

Notice at the same time that Antichrist goes after God's people, these two witnesses are right in the middle of the fray in Jerusalem, prophesying and declaring the truth of God in defiance of the Antichrist. So furious is Antichrist against these two servants of God that he actively tries to kill them. But God protects them supernaturally and they cannot be harmed, until their work is over.

IT ALL ADDS UP TO DANIEL'S LAST SEVEN YEARS

Notice the adjoining chart and we can see how Daniel's two actions of Antichrist align themselves with key prophecies in both the Olivet Prophecy and the book of Revelation. There is a symmetry of events, which insists upon a seven year time span to fulfill, from the arrival of Antichrist to the arrival of the true Messiah!

THE SYMMETRY OF
DANIEL'S PROPHESIED LAST 7 YEARS

DANIEL	7 SEALS	JESUS
ANTICHRIST CONFIRMS COVENANT (Dan 9:27)	**1** WHITE HORSE FALSE CHRISTS (Rev 6:1-2)	FALSE CHRISTS (Matt 24:4-5)
3½ YEARS	**2** RED HORSE WAR (Rev 6:3-4)	WAR (Matt 24:6-7)
	3 BLACK HORSE FAMINE (Rev 6:5-6)	FAMINE (Matt 24:7)
	4 PALE HORSE DEATH (Rev 6:7-8)	SORROWS (Matt 24:8)
ANTICHRIST BREAKS COVENANT (Dan 9:27)	**5** GREAT TRIBULATION (Rev 6:9-11)	GREAT TRIBULATION (Matt 24:15-22)
3½ YEARS	**6** SIGNS IN SUN, MOON, STARS (Rev 6:12-17)	SIGNS IN SUN, MOON, STARS (Matt 24:29)
RAPTURE	(Rev 7:9-17)	(Matt 24:29-31)
CHRIST RETURNS	**7** DAY OF THE LORD (Rev 6:17-9:21)	DAY OF THE LORD (Matt 24:30)

This book has attempted to lay out a biblical timeframe of end-time events which cannot be debated. Let's review the timeline now. Jesus speaks of the first three and a half years between the Antichrist confirming and then breaking the covenant as the beginning of sorrows in Matthew 24:8. That time represents the effects of Antichrist, war, famine, and death that the four horsemen bring – all of which precede the three and a half years of the Great Tribulation.

The Great Tribulation is *not* the wrath of God, neither is it the return of Jesus. The wrath of God and His return are on the Day of the Lord. Notice seals five and seven are separated by the sixth seal (signs in the sun, moon and stars). **God has purposely separated these two seals so that there can be no confusion about the matter. And it is this false teaching that says they are both the same thing that has brought about so much confusion in the body of Christ.** We have seen that the Great Tribulation is Satan's wrath against God's people and all mankind (Rev 12:12). It becomes so severe that Jesus Himself says He has to cut short those days for the elect's sake. They are still on the earth and they haven't been raptured yet! That certainly throws a monkey wrench into the eschatology taught by many today!

Some would argue that the rapture had already taken place for the Church and that these *elect* became Christians *after* the rapture. Then are there *two* raptures? And are the dead in Christ going to be resurrected *twice*?

Unfortunately, their arguments do nothing to prepare a people to withstand the tough days ahead.

In the adjoining chart, you'll also notice that Christ's return to earth completes not only Daniel's last week prophecy, but also the entire 70 week prophecy.

Seventy weeks are determined upon thy people and upon thy holy city, to finish the transgression, and to make an end of sins, and to make reconciliation for iniquity, and to bring in everlasting righteousness, and to seal up the vision and prophecy, and to anoint the most Holy (Dan 9:24).

Yes, Jesus finishes the transgression. Jesus makes an end of sin. Jesus makes reconciliation for iniquity. Jesus brings in everlasting righteousness. And, Jesus anoints the most Holy with His presence on earth. Now the Kingdom of God reigns on earth, overthrowing all other kingdoms.

WINDOW OF OPPORTUNITY

Armed with this teaching, we can be better equipped in rejecting false prognostications of rapture date settings and warnings of impeding doom and gloom. We're better able to dismiss the constant refrains we hear so often of 'the countdown has already begun!" or the "Red Horse of war has already begun riding."

All of these dire but false warnings only position the Body of Christ in a perpetual defensive manner, keeping us impotent as we anxiously await the next shoe to drop as we only keep our eyes focused on escaping this earth. Meanwhile we should be advancing the Kingdom of God on the earth *until* His return. And if we believe Christ's return is imminent, then it's all the more reason to work for Him with increasing fervor while it is day. The night comes when no one can work (Jn 9:4).

In the past we've seen Christ's admonition of wars and rumors of wars and antichrists, etc, as something we've always had for millennia. And that's true. But when you understand that Christ's prophecies are bound to a short time span of seven years, then everything makes sense.

Daniel's last seven years only begin when Antichrist confirms a covenant in Israel. Then there will be an uninterrupted march of seven years of fulfilled prophecies that cannot be prayed away.

So please don't get carried away with every news event purportedly fulfilling the end times. Of course, things are leading up to Christ's return, but the ultimate news event to watch out for is the Antichrist confirming a covenant in Israel to reestablish Temple worship.

Until that happens, we are free to pursue all that the Lord has destined for our lives! Don't let the fear of end-time events short circuit your drive, calling and destiny.

As we've said before, Daniel's last seven years are not fixed in scripture to a certain date. It is Seals on Wheels, and God is the only One who will determine when to begin that timeline. Until that time happens, we can and should be praying on behalf of the nation. We should pray that America repents, that it turns back to God, that God have mercy on us all, that the waves of satanic legislation coming from Washington be rescinded, that Christians the world over be protected, and that life from the womb to old age is protected. We should pray that America is awakened to truth and righteousness again.

Did you know that America, in its history, has experienced two major Awakenings that lasted for *decades?* And they occurred *before* national tragedies!

The first Awakening was before America even became a nation. From the time the Mayflower brought its occupants to these shores, we have been dedicating this land to God through our Lord Jesus Christ. Civil laws were based on scripture. The impact of this Awakening became the foundation of our laws, the Declaration of Independence and the Constitution. The freedoms we enjoy today were all predicated on our God-centered foundations.

Yet the fledgling Nation was almost aborted upon its inception with freedom of religion hanging in the balance as Great Britain sought to stop our fight for independence.

The second major Awakening to hit the United States, which also lasted for decades, was just before the Civil War.

How long will this next Awakening last before disaster strikes? It could be decades, as well.

So now is not the time to give up hope and recede into apathy and ineffectiveness. Jesus commands His followers to occupy till He comes! (Lk 19:13). Right now, more than any other time, we ought to be excelling in the fruits and gifts of the Holy Spirit and fulfill the very destiny that God has called us to achieve. God has allowed us to be living at a most pivotal time in all creation. Therefore God has a purpose for our lives, to do something challenging and rewarding, and, even in the face of prevailing evil, to literally be strong and do exploits! (Dan 11:32).

Now is the time to become ever more vigilant in defending truth and exposing evil. *Cry aloud, spare not, lift up thy voice like a trumpet and show My people their sins and the House of Jacob their transgression* (Isa 58:1).

We are to maintain our positions on the wall, even in battling ominous threats coming upon the earth, even in engaging the enemy who would seek to bring the nations to their knees before their time. Should a movement come afoot to bring martial law in America, so long as Antichrist has not confirmed the covenant in Israel, I'm praying and fighting against it! Should the liberals continue the push for abortion, open borders, and reducing America's strength, both morally and militarily, I'm praying and fighting against it. Should globalists push their one world government with fake scares of global warming and climate change, I'm praying and fighting against it.

The whole point of this section of teaching is to show that Daniel's last seven years have not yet begun! Therefore, let us do all we can in God's power to defend truth and righteousness and carry out all that God has commissioned us to do.

God can begin the seven year timeline whenever He chooses. But, is it possible, that so long as His people are carrying out His will and turning this world "right side up" with the gospel, making great strides in evangelizing nations and saving lost mankind, God will hold back end-time events till He sees fit? God's heart, after all, is on the lost. And He desires His people to have a heart like His.

But once Daniel's last seven years begin, there is no way to pray for anymore delays. Everything prophesied will occur rapidly, though you could still pray for individual and family safety and salvation during the Great Tribulation. But until that happens, we must continue being the stewards of God upon the earth, proclaiming God's truth and revelations, and carrying out exploits with the power of the Holy Spirit to a hurt and dying world. The harvest now is bigger than ever before and that should be our paramount aim.

In the next chapter, we will move to a section of scripture that adds more details to Daniel's timeline and to Antichrist, in particular.

7
ANTICHRIST WARS

And I stood upon the sand of the sea, and saw a beast rise up out of the sea, having seven heads and ten horns, and upon his horns ten crowns, and upon his heads the name of blasphemy. And the beast which I saw was like unto a leopard, and his feet were as the feet of a bear, and his mouth as the mouth of a lion: and the dragon gave him his power, and his seat, and great authority... And they worshipped the dragon which gave power unto the beast: **and they worshipped the beast, saying, Who is like unto the beast? who is able to make war with him?** (Rev 13:1-2, 4).*

This is the bizarre, nearly incomprehensible, biblical description of the Antichrist: seven heads, ten horns, leopard, bear, lion, dragon, etc. What could all this mean? Yet it's important for us to understand what it means because this strange beast, representing the Antichrist, causes great destruction upon the world and demands that all the nations submit to him. He receives this worldwide acclaim because of his military prowess: *who is able to make war with him?*

By the time you finish this chapter on *Antichrist Wars*, you will understand the meaning of the symbols of this beast and you will see how it all ties in with Daniel's seven year timeline and the seals of Revelation.

We have outlined our position that the Antichrist confirms a covenant to restore Jewish Temple worship upon the most hotly contested parcel of land in the world – Jerusalem's Temple Mount.

Can you imagine the Arab outrage around the world as soon as this happens? The scriptures show us that war breaks out as soon as this covenant is signed as Arab nations attack the State of Israel. Even if one has the most rudimentary geopolitical knowledge, one can easily see how all this can play out in the most natural progression.

The first seal is the appearance of Antichrist, who reacts to this massive Arab attack against him by *going forth conquering and to conquer.* The second seal, that naturally follows, is war breaking out in the Middle East. The third seal is famine, which is the natural outcome of war. Then the fourth seal shows us that, even before the Great Tribulation begins, the Antichrist has one forth of the world under his control.

The scriptures chronicle, step by step, Antichrist's rise to power, his sweep of Arab neighbors, and his conquest of the world.

Daniel 7 and 11, for instance, are two vitally important corroborating passages of scripture to Revelation 13. They detail the early wars of Antichrist and explain why the beast of Revelation is depicted as various animal symbols. All of this fits in with the period of time that Jesus refers to as the *beginning of sorrows* (the three and a half years *before* the Great Tribulation).

Daniel was given a horrifying and revealing end-time dream in Daniel 7, which is for our understanding today.

In the first year of Belshazzar king of Babylon Daniel had a dream and visions of his head upon his bed:

then he wrote the dream, and told the sum of the matters. Daniel spake and said, I saw in my vision by night, and, behold, the four winds of the heaven strove upon the great sea. And four great beasts came up from the sea, diverse one from another (Dan 7:1-3).

It's important to clarify that this dream is not in any way a retelling of the dream that Nebuchadnezzar had in chapter two. This is a totally different dream given for a totally different purpose. For instance, Nebuchadnezzar's dream in chapter two consists of a large statue made up of different metals depicting world empires that would come upon the scene in sequential order, one right after the other, leading up to the return of Jesus Christ.

In Daniel 7, however, the beasts that arise do so contemporaneously just before Christ's return. They appear *suddenly* on the world's scenes. Daniel 7:12 later suggests that these kingdoms do, indeed, arise at the same time.

Furthermore, the Aramaic word for *strove* (as in *the four winds of heaven strove against the great sea*) suggests a *bursting forth.* Therefore these empires or confederation of nations aren't even apparent on the world's scene today, as they are yet to burst forth. Daniel 11 hints to us their identities, as we shall see as we compare scripture with scripture. We propose that they burst forth suddenly on the world's scene as a direct military response to the Antichrist instituting Temple worship on the Temple Mount!

Now let's notice something about the four beasts in Daniel's dream and how it applies to the Antichrist beast of Revelation 13.

The first was like a lion, and had eagle's wings: I beheld till the wings thereof were plucked, and it was lifted up from the earth, and made stand upon the feet as a man, and a man's heart was given to it. And behold another beast, a second, like to a bear, and it raised up itself on one side, and it had three ribs in the mouth of it between the teeth of it: and they said thus unto it, Arise, devour much flesh. After this I beheld, and lo another, like a leopard, which had upon the back of it four wings of a fowl; the beast had also four heads; and dominion was given to it. After this I saw in the night visions, and behold a fourth beast, dreadful and terrible, and strong exceedingly; and it had great iron teeth: it devoured and brake in pieces, and stamped the residue with the feet of it: and it was diverse from all the beasts that were before it; and it had ten horns. I considered the horns, and, behold, there came up among them another little horn, before whom there were three of the first horns plucked up by the roots: and, behold, in this horn were eyes like the eyes of man, and a mouth speaking great things (Dan 7:4-8).

Notice that the beast of Revelation 13 is the exact composite of the four beasts in Daniel 7. The beast of Revelation has seven heads and ten horns, with attributes of a lion, bear, and leopard, as does Daniel's four beasts combined. And both scriptures center around the Antichrist. God is telling us something.

What we're seeing here in Daniel 7 are the four nations or groups of nations that are eventually absorbed into the Antichrist beast power by the start of the Great Tribulation.

Charles Cooper, former professor of Hermeneutics at Moody Bible Institute and proponent of the pre-wrath rapture position, makes the compelling case, with which we agree, that the empires in Daniel 7 represent the same empires in Daniel 11. And just as Daniel 7 suggests that the empires come out of the *four winds* (i.e., North, East, South, and West), Daniel 11 also speaks of kings coming out of the points of a compass. Each chapter seems to give additional information on each empire.

Therefore we will examine chapters seven and eleven,

side by side, and present our best assessment on each point. The exact identities for each empire will only be fully understood when the time comes. But scripture gives us enough information to reach at a starting point.

THE KING OF THE SOUTH

The first was like a lion, and had eagle's wings: I beheld till the wings thereof were plucked, and it was lifted up from the earth, and made stand upon the feet as a man, and a man's heart was given to it (Dan 7:4)

*And at the time of the end shall the **king of the south push at him**: and the king of the north shall come against him like a whirlwind, with chariots, and with horsemen, and with many ships; and he shall enter into the countries, and shall overflow and pass over* (Dan 11:40).

What the above verses show us is that this first empire is swift and strong at the beginning (*like a lion, and had eagle's wings*). It is also the first empire to attack the Antichrist and, conversely, the first to be humbled by the Antichrist (*wings plucked).* Daniel 11:40 assures us of the Antichrist's victory over the King of the South as he *shall enter into the countries and shall overflow and pass over.* The King's initial fierce lion's heart (*bold as a lion,* Pro 28:1) is reduced to a lowly man's heart. It's likely that the King of the South, using Jerusalem as the center compass point, is Egypt (Dan 11:42-43).

The scriptures preceding Daniel 11:40 refer to an earlier prophetic time involving Antiochus Epiphanes, the forerunner to the end-time Antichrist. Yet, quite often, scripture suddenly morphs from types to realities within verses. This is just such a case. Verse 40 brings us up to date with the phrase: *at the time of the end* and refers to the coming Antichrist.

The king of the south shall push at him, we maintain, refers to the military response the King initiates against Israel for reestablishing temple worship.

THE KING OF THE NORTH

*And behold **another beast, a second, like to a bear,** and it raised up itself on one side, and it had three ribs in the mouth of it between the teeth of it: and they said thus unto it, Arise, devour much flesh* (Dan 7:5)

*And at the time of the end shall the king of the south push at him: and the **king of the north** shall come against him like a whirlwind, with chariots, and with horsemen, and with many ships; and he shall enter into the countries, and shall overflow and pass over* (Dan 11:40).

Many preachers of eschatology have always assumed that the King of the North is Russia. But we've found, quite often, that many over the years have mistakenly attributed biblical symbols to the then current political bogeyman – Russia being one of the chief perennial bogeymen. Yet, coincidentally enough, this second beast is a *bear*, and Russian symbolism *is* a bear. But for this point to hold true, all the other nations should also be officially symbolized by their biblical animal types as well, and they don't.

Judging from the fact that this *beast like a bear* had three ribs in its mouth, we can conclude that this beast envelops three other territories and they work together in tandem against the Antichrist. Charles Cooper suggests that this King of the North is therefore a confederation of Northern Arab countries.

The last verse has caused some confusion over the word *he*. Who's the *he* who *enters into the countries, overflows and passes over?*

Some believe *he* refers to the King of the North. We maintain that *he* refers to the Antichrist, as we can plainly see when we follow the scriptures' train of thought in the next few verses: (41) *he* shall return to the glorious land (modern state of Israel); (42) *he* shall overrun countries, such as Egypt; (43) *he* shall take possession of the booty of Egypt; (44) *he* shall respond militarily to threats from the King of the North (that's checkmate right there!); (45) he shall plant himself (as god) in the glorious land (i.e., Jerusalem, *between the seas*: Mediterranean and Galilee).

Therefore the *he* can only be the Antichrist that militarily responds against the attacks and enters *into the countries, overflows and passes over.*

Incidentally, as you can plainly see, this *he* will display an extraordinary military prowess! Despite flanking attacks from north and south, we again read in Daniel 11:40 that the Antichrist vanquishes both armies, somewhat reminiscent of the Six Day War.

Deception is the hallmark of the end times and when this Jewish Antichrist protects Israel in a manner just like the spectacular victories of modern Israel's past, can you begin to see how many well-meaning Christians and others will support his victories? This will ironically prove to be Satan's most cunningly devised strategy to make the world approve of the military conquests of Antichrist and to blind it to his true intentions.

Many have been confused thinking that the Antichrist is a non-Jewish outsider fighting *against* Israel. But he will, in fact, be a Jewish military leader fighting on behalf of Israel.

As an aside, some who maintain that the Antichrist is non-Jewish point to this scripture:

> *He shall enter also into the glorious land, and many*
> *countries shall be overthrown: but these shall escape*
> *out of his hand, even Edom, and Moab, and the chief*
> *of the children of Ammon* (Dan 11:41).

They say that this foreign Antichrist enters into the *glorious land* (Israel) and takes over the region. We counter by saying that after Antichrist's victory abroad he seeks to clean house within Israel's own borders and the so-called Occupied Territories, for at that time there will be no international force strong enough to prevent Israel from taking full control of its disputed areas.

Edom, Moab and Ammon form the area today known as Jordan, which, interestingly, *escapes out of his hand.* How Jordan escapes out of Antichrist's hands will be made plain once the time arrives. Nevertheless, the indication is that Jordan will become a place of refuge that God will prepare for those still living in Israel to escape the soon-coming wrath of Antichrist. When Christ says to *flee,* in Matthew 24, Jordan may just be the nearby place to flee to!

And when the time comes, we will find that there will be many other places of refuge around the world that the Lord will provide for His people during the Great Tribulation.

THE KING(S) OF THE EAST

*After this I beheld, and **lo another, like a leopard,** which had upon the back of it four wings of a fowl; the beast had also **four heads;** and dominion was given to it* (Dan 7:6)

*But **tidings out of the east** and out of the north shall trouble him: therefore he shall go forth with great fury to destroy, and utterly to make away many* (Dan 11:44).

What we find here is that the King(s) of the East are composed of four main heads who will spontaneously arise once the time comes. The news, or tidings, from these kings and the King of the North seem to threaten the Antichrist, and once again he goes forth *with great fury to destroy them.*

THE KING(S) OF THE WEST

*After this I saw in the night visions, and behold a **fourth beast, dreadful and terrible**, and strong exceedingly; and it had great iron teeth: it devoured and brake in pieces, and stamped the residue with the feet of it: and it was diverse from all the beasts that were before it; and it had ten horns. I considered the horns, and, behold, there came up among them another little horn, before whom there were three of the first horns plucked up by the roots: and, behold, in this horn were eyes like the eyes of man, and a mouth speaking great things* (Dan 7:7-8).

And, so we come to the ultimate beast, the one that was diverse from all the others, the one that encapsulates Antichrist's crowning achievement of global domination. The beast that was far more oppressive than the others.

While Daniel 11 does not have a corresponding beast reference to the above verse, we can reasonably conclude that this reference is to nations arising out of Europe.

With each new conquest, Antichrist will push the world closer and closer to the Great Tribulation. The full strength and authority of the beast of Revelation 13 occurs only *after* all of Daniel's four beasts have been subjugated.

What the above verses tell us is that this terrible beast was the strongest of all. *It devoured and brake in pieces, and stamped the residue with the feet of it*, meaning, in essence, that whatever the other three beasts did not or could not devour (*the residue*), this fourth beast did.

It also shows us that there are ten horns on this fourth beast. Then another horn (the Antichrist) appears among them. He *plucks up by the roots* three of the ten horns. What this tells us is that Antichrist topples three of the ten kings, thus ensuring his dominance in that empire.

In summary, what we're seeing throughout this chapter is the fulfillment of the first two seals of Revelation: the rise of

Antichrist and the proliferation of wars. Daniel 7 shows us the military campaigns that will strategically advance the Antichrist's domination of the world in time for the Great Tribulation.

There are also some positive details to glean from in Daniel 7, so let's continue on with the chapter. We see that Antichrist's hold on the world is only short lived, as Jesus returns to destroy the Antichrist and to set up His Kingdom.

I beheld till the thrones were cast down, and the Ancient of days did sit, whose garment was white as snow, and the hair of his head like the pure wool: his throne was like the fiery flame, and his wheels as burning fire. A fiery stream issued and came forth from before him: thousand thousands ministered unto him, and ten thousand times ten thousand stood before him: the judgment was set, and the books were opened. I beheld then because of the voice of the great words which the horn spake: **I beheld even till the beast was slain, and his body destroyed, and given to the burning flame** (Dan 7:9-11).

The Antichrist will be tossed into the burning flame, which is the lake of fire (Rev 19:20).

I saw in the night visions, and, behold, one like the Son of man came with the clouds of heaven, and came to the Ancient of days, and they brought him near before him. And there was given him dominion, and glory, and a kingdom, that all people, nations, and languages, should serve him: his dominion is an everlasting dominion, which shall not pass away, and his kingdom that which shall not be destroyed (Dan 7:13-14).

Here we see the Son of man (Jesus Christ) appearing before the Ancient of Days (the Father) as the Kingdom is again returned to the Father and now given to the saints for their inheritance. As we continue in chapter seven, more details about the final beast and related issues are given.

MORE DETAILS ABOUT THE BEAST

I Daniel was grieved in my spirit in the midst of my body, and the visions of my head troubled me. I came near unto one of them that stood by, and asked him the truth of all this. So he told me, and made me know the interpretation of the things. ***These great beasts, which are four, are four kings, which shall arise out of the earth. But the saints of the most High shall take the kingdom, and possess the kingdom for ever, even for ever and ever*** (Dan 7:15-18).

Daniel, troubled in every way, petitioned the angels for more details and one of them gave him only scant more details, including the fact that each beast represented a king. Then, in an attempt to assuage Daniel's grief, the angel emphasized that the saints were going to be the rightful inheritors of the kingdoms of this world and rule forever. But Daniel, still troubled, wanted to know more about the most dreadful beast of all, the fourth one.

Then I would know the truth of the fourth beast, which was diverse from all the others, exceeding dreadful, whose teeth were of iron, and his nails of brass; which devoured, brake in pieces, and stamped the residue with his feet; And of the ten horns that were in his head, and of the other which came up, and before whom three fell; even of that horn that had eyes, and a mouth that spake very great things, whose look was more stout than his fellows. ***I beheld, and the same horn made war with the saints, and prevailed against them;*** *Until the Ancient of days came, and judgment was given to the saints of the most High; and the time came that the saints possessed the kingdom* (Dan 7:19-22).

Now Daniel offers another insight to the vision. The Antichrist also wars against the saints of God, and *prevails over them*. If you've been reading up till now, you'll know that this corresponds to the Great Tribulation. And all of what we're detailing consistently proves the inerrancy of Daniel's seven year timeframe, coupled with the rest of the eschatological scriptures.

> *Thus he said, The fourth beast shall be the fourth kingdom upon earth, which shall be diverse from all kingdoms, and shall devour the whole earth, and shall tread it down, and break it in pieces. And the ten horns out of this kingdom are ten kings that shall arise: and another shall rise after them; and he shall be diverse from the first, and he shall subdue three kings.* **And he shall speak great words against the most High, and shall wear out the saints of the most High, and think to change times and laws: and they shall be given into his hand until a time and times and the dividing of time.** *But the judgment shall sit, and they shall take away his dominion, to consume and to destroy it unto the end. And the kingdom and dominion, and the greatness of the kingdom under the whole heaven, shall be given to the people of the saints of the most High, whose kingdom is an everlasting kingdom, and all dominions shall serve and obey him* (Dan 7:23-27).

What a powerful summary of the last diverse kingdom, through which the Antichrist will rule over all the world. Once this last fourth beast or kingdom comes under Antichrist's control, the beast of Revelation 13 takes center stage in the world, complete with the persecution of the saints of God. For good reason Jesus said that as soon as the Antichrist enters the temple professing that he is god, the people of God should scatter and find refuge from Antichrist (Mt 24:15-22).

The good news is, of course, that this is only temporary and that soon the saints are given power, judgment and authority over the world in the coming Millennium, and beyond.

You'll notice in the above verse that the Antichrist attempts to *change times and laws.* Lots of speculation surrounds this verse, but whatever it means, it must refer to the persecuted saints, since it's sandwiched between two clauses dealing specifically with them. The phrase *time, times and the dividing of time*, of course, means it's talking about the Great Tribulation. Is it an attempt to change the times and laws dealing with three and a half years of persecuting the saints? Does Satan, through the Antichrist, want to prolong the time? Jesus had already stated that the three and a half years of the Great Tribulation were actually going to be shortened (Mt 24:22). We're merely presenting this as a possible scenario. We'll know for certain when the time comes.

WHERE'S AMERICA?

One of the most vigorously debated topics is the whereabouts of the United States of America in the end times. There are end-time references in the Bible to several smaller countries, so why are the scriptures seemingly silent about perhaps the most influential Christian nation of all time? On the other hand, when teachers *do* mention America in scripture, it's usually tied into a condescending reference to Mystery Babylon!

This topic deserves its own volume and therefore we will not be able to do it justice here. However, we will simply say that the United States will be in no position to resist or stop the demonically empowered Antichrist during Daniel's last seven years.

If the reader desires further information about America in prophecy, please refer to my own video entitled, *"Mindshift:*

America in Prophecy," on my News2morrow YouTube channel.

WHERE'S THE CHURCH?

With so much fear and dread over the end times, we can understand why there is so much support for a pre-tribulation rapture. We know the Antichrist will have *total* control over the earth – which is what Satan had wanted all along – militarily, economically and religiously. It will be the globalists' One World Government they've always dreamed of.

It's far more appealing to embrace the idea that the Church won't be around for the Antichrist, but as we've found out in scripture the Church is *still* on the earth when Antichrist appears (2 Thess 2:3, Mt 24:15-22, Dan 7:21, 25, Rev 12:17, 13:7).

Yet each year we find some ministry or some YouTube sensation setting new dates for the rapture. Each date comes in like a whirlwind and goes out like a corpse's last breath.

We're trying to conclude each of these chapters with an encouragement to reject false alarms of rapture date-setting and instead turn one's attention to our own God-ordained work at hand. There is a world to conquer for the Kingdom. Jesus said, *Greater works shall **you** do* (Jn 14:12) – that means even greater than what Christ had done!

Has anyone of us achieved that level of power? So, why would we be content to escape this world now, not having done anything of meaningful importance for the Kingdom? What sort of reward do you think we're going to get?

We hope this volume equips you with the truth so that you don't get so easily sidetracked by every prognosticator's end-time decree on social media.

Armed with this truth, you can stop seeking ways to escape this world and shirking your present duties. **These fake dates are distractions to the Body of Christ to keep you in a perpetual mindset of flight, to avoid you fulfilling your God-ordained destiny right here on earth.** That's Satan's strategy, isn't it? An escapist mentality distracts you from the works that Christ wants you to perform now!

Jesus said, *Occupy till I come!* (Lk 19:13). Jesus may not yet come for decades still. Shouldn't we consider that while we're waiting for His return, there is still an awakening to take place in America and the world? And we've been given the invitation by being born at this time to be a part of the Church's greatest era! Rather than being breathless to get out of here, let's be breathless to do the greater works of God.

Where are the Moses' of today to deliver His people out of bondage? Where are the Elijahs? The Davids? The apostles who could turn the world right side up?

Where are the Deborahs? The Mordechais? Where are the battalions storming the gates of hell? Where is God's advancing army, or are they quivering to flee like defeated grasshoppers (Num 13:33)?

It's high time the Church arose to its rightful position to change the corrupted culture in our lands, to defend truth and justice, to speak out – until *victory* – for the 60 million-plus aborted children. What we've seen instead is that the culture has intimidated the Christians. It seems that gays came out of the closet and Christians went into it!

Cry aloud, spare not, lift up thy voice like a trumpet and show My people their transgressions and the House of Jacob their sins (Isa 58:1). Try to find ways to offer the gospel perspective to a hurt, deceived and dying world, in ways they can embrace and understand.

Friends, let's not squander the potential that the Lord Jesus Himself has bestowed upon each and every one of us.

To anyone willing to die to self and to man's opinions, Jesus is willing to empower that person to fulfill his or her commission to make a major impact on this world that, up till now, we've given up on.

Greater works shall *you* do! Let's not hightail out of here until we do!

8
OTHER MARKS OF THE BEAST

We've seen already the main characteristic of Antichrist as a warmonger. He is known for war and, with the help of Satan, he defeats enough nations to take control of the entire world, militarily, economically and spiritually. He even makes war against the saints (Dan 7:21, Rev 13:7)! You've heard that the Antichrist will be known by the mysterious symbol of 666 (Rev 13:18). But there are other characteristics that we'd now like to review.

One of the main points we're trying to make in this entire volume is to show how deceptive the Antichrist will be in imitating the real Christ. Satan's best strategy has always been to counterfeit whatever God does.

Ancient Israel expected the Messiah to wage war against Israel's enemies, and Antichrist fulfills that promise to a tee.

Therefore it is not surprising that Satan would also imitate Christ's greatest supernatural sign of His Messiahship – His Resurrection (Mt 12:39-40).

ANTICHRIST RISES FROM THE DEAD

There is a pivotal time in Antichrist's military campaign when he receives a mortal head wound from either war injuries or an assassination attempt. And it's at that time, we believe, that Satan enters him, more so than at the first, and empowers him to complete his diabolical work ahead.

There are several scriptures that point to this. Let's try to follow them in as close a chronological fashion as possible. We've seen in the last chapter that the Antichrist goes on a military campaign *conquering and to conquer*, as the first seal describes his actions. Then we read this:

> *And he shall plant the tabernacles of his palace between the seas in the glorious holy mountain;* **yet he shall come to his end, and none shall help him** (Dan 11:45).

Following his victorious campaign, conquering the other heads that make up the composite beast of Revelation 13, we now see that he plants himself firmly in Jerusalem, the *holy mountain*, as Daniel 9:16 calls it.

There is an interesting phrase in the above verse: *yet he shall come to his end, and none shall help him.* The text seems to suggest that he died suddenly. But that can't be since, at this point, the Great Tribulation hasn't even begun yet. The Antichrist has much more work to do!

A clue can be found in the following chapter. So let's disregard the inappropriately placed chapter break and read on:

> *And at that time shall Michael stand up, the great prince which standeth for the children of thy people:* **and there shall be a time of trouble, such as never was since there was a nation even to that same time:** *and at that time thy people shall be delivered, every one that shall be found written in the book* (Dan 12:1).

We should be familiar with this verse by now. It's the verse that precipitates the Great Tribulation. It's the verse that shows Michael the Archangel standing up to remove Satan first from heaven and soon thereafter from earth (Rev 20:1-3). Michael is the restraining agent that protects the children of God.

We've already shown that Antichrist will immediately demand the world's worship at the start of the Great Tribulation. But how can that happen if the Antichrist already *came to his end* in the previous verse with none being able to *help him?* Putting scripture to scripture, we can conclude that once Satan is ejected from heaven that he immediately enters the Antichrist anew, in an apparent resurrection.

But we're getting ahead of ourselves. Let's first backtrack a bit to show other scriptures that detail this head wound.

> *And I stood upon the sand of the sea, and saw a beast rise up out of the sea, having seven heads and ten horns, and upon his horns ten crowns, and upon his heads the name of blasphemy. And the beast which I saw was like unto a leopard, and his feet were as the feet of a bear, and his mouth as the mouth of a lion: and the dragon gave him his power, and his seat, and great authority.* **And I saw one of his heads as it were wounded to death; and his deadly wound was healed: and all the world wondered after the beast.** *And they worshipped the dragon which gave power unto the beast: and they worshipped the beast, saying, Who is like unto the beast? who is able to make war with him?* (Rev 13:1-4).

Some critics argue that this *deadly wound* couldn't be referring to any physical man since he'd have to have six other heads.

Well, we've seen in the previous chapter that the Antichrist is a composite of seven national heads, or regions. While verse four above affirms that the beast is a *he* (*who is able to make war with him?*).

There are some who attribute the deadly wound to a government which ceased to exist and then, miraculously, is restored. But why would the *world wonder* about a government that arises again? It's far more credible for the world to wonder about a human being who dies and then is resurrected. To debate against Antichrist's *deadly wound* in this fashion is to reject other scriptures as well. A few verses later, we read (speaking of the False Prophet):

> *And* (he) *deceiveth them that dwell on the earth by the means of those miracles which he had power to do in the sight of the beast; saying to them that dwell on the earth, that **they should make an image to the beast, which had the wound by a sword, and did live*** (Rev 13:14).

A *sword* wound is usually symbolic of a military wound, as in *he who lives by the sword shall die by the sword* (Rev 13:10).

A seldom used scripture that also attests to the Antichrist's head wound is this one from the Old Testament:

> *For, lo, I will raise up a shepherd in the land, which shall not visit those that be cut off, neither shall seek the young one, nor heal that that is broken, nor feed that that standeth still: but he shall eat the flesh of the fat, and tear their claws in pieces. Woe to the idol shepherd that leaveth the flock! **the sword shall be upon his arm, and upon his right eye: his arm shall be clean dried up, and his right eye shall be utterly darkened*** (Zech 11:16-17).

So we now have more information about Antichrist's mortal wound. It not only affects his head, but more specifically he loses vision in his right eye. Plus, his right arm will be paralyzed as well. It sounds like he was caught up in an explosion of some sort.

But when this near death episode rebounds to a seemingly miraculous resurrection, the world will take notice and be in *wonderment!* The Greek word used for *wondered* doesn't necessarily mean to *wonder*, as in questioning. For this *wondered* means to *marvel*, to *admire*, to *hold in admiration* – for these are the building blocks for worship.

Again, this cannot be talking about an old government coming back to life. It has to refer to an apparent resurrection of a previously dead, or near as dead, individual.

This naturally begs the question: can Satan raise the dead?

No, we would suspect not. But we do know that Satan can cause injuries and maladies upon people that come close to an appearance of death. And all he has to do to feign a resurrection is to remove the illness that he put upon him. And the Antichrist will appear to be made well.

You'll note, to use a non-demonic example, that even the Apostle Paul appeared dead to others after he was stoned by persecutors, yet he recovered (Acts 14:19).

So however it's done, whatever trick is used, it certainly appears to the world to be a genuine resurrection – enough for Satan to deceive the world.

But getting back to an earlier point we made; there is strong indication that once Satan is forcibly ejected from heaven, he not only comes down to earth having great wrath but he *possesses* the Antichrist more fully, making him more a child of Satan than ever.

We propose that it's at this very time that he empowers the Antichrist to proclaim himself as god, demanding worship from the world (Rev 12:7-9, 13; Dan 9:27, 12:1; 2 Thess 2:4, 6-8).

The fact that the Antichrist miraculously rises from the dead is the physical "proof" for the False Prophet to compel the world to worship the self-proclaimed god – the Antichrist.

The "resurrection" is such an identifying hallmark of the beast that the scriptures have a term for it.

HE WAS, IS NOT, AND YET IS

This paradoxical biblical title, repeatedly given to the Antichrist, symbolizes the "miracle" of his rising from the dead.

1) *The beast that was, and is not, and yet is,* Rev 17:8
2) *The beast was, and is not, and shall ascend out of the bottomless pit and go into perdition,* Rev 17:8
3) *And the beast that was, and is not, even he is the eighth, and is of the seven, and goes into perdition,* Rev 17:11
4) *The first beast, whose deadly wound was healed,* Rev 13:12
5) *The beast, which had the wound by a sword, and did live,* Rev 13:14
6) *The beast that ascended out of the bottomless pit,* Rev 11:7

The *bottomless pit* is an interesting term. It comes from the Greek word for *abyssos,* rendered as *abyss* in other translations, and as *bottomless, bottomless pit* and *deep* in the King James Version.

The term depicts a resurrection from the dead, as in this verse:

> *But the righteousness which is of faith speaketh on this wise, Say not in thine heart, Who shall ascend into heaven? (that is, to bring Christ down from above:) Or, Who shall descend into the **deep?** [abyssos] (that is, to bring up Christ again from the dead.)* (Rom 10:6-7).

Therefore, the same Greek word designating Christ's Resurrection is also likened to the Antichrist's resurrection. And, similarly, the same title that Antichrist (Satan) attempts to appropriate for himself is how the Lord describes Himself:

I am he that liveth, and was dead; and, behold, I am alive for evermore (Rev 1:18).

We are going to be experiencing interesting times ahead, my friends. Therefore, be on guard. The enemy will pull out all the stops to deceive the people, yet God promises an end to the Antichrist.

As an aside, both the Antichrist and Judas are each called the *son of perdition* (Jn 17:12; 2 Thess 2:3). And perdition (i.e., the lake of fire) is where they will both reside forever (Rev 17:11, 19:20).

But there's more. Not only will the Antichrist imitate Christ's Resurrection from the dead, he will also perform many miracles to further deceive the world.

ASSOCIATED WITH MIRACLES

But there was a certain man, called Simon, which beforetime in the same city used sorcery, and bewitched the people of Samaria, giving out that himself was some great one: To whom they all gave heed, from the least to the greatest, saying, This man is the great power of God. And to him they had regard, because that of long time he had bewitched them with sorceries (Acts 8:9-11).

Satan can imitate genuine miracles of God to confuse the populace. Simon did here, and he received acclaim as if he was doing it by the power of God. The magicians at the time of Moses also duplicated the miracles of God. And so will the Antichrist (by the way, that resurrection miracle was pretty impressive, wasn't it?).

*And then shall that Wicked be revealed, whom the Lord shall consume with the spirit of his mouth, and shall destroy with the brightness of his coming: **Even him, whose coming is after the working of Satan***

125

with all power and signs and lying wonders, And with all deceivableness of unrighteousness in them that perish; because they received not the love of the truth, that they might be saved. And for this cause God shall send them strong delusion, that they should believe a lie (2 Thess 2:8-11).

Yes, Satan will empower his son, the Antichrist, with demonic miracles, sorceries, signs and lying wonders. Revelation 16:14 declares that it is the *spirits of devils* that are *working miracles*. And it's interesting that the original Greek word used here denoting demonic *miracles* is the same word used when describing the *miracles* of God (as in Jn 2:11, *the beginning of miracles which did Jesus in Cana of Galilee*).

The lie, we maintain is the lie that the Antichrist is God or the Messiah.

Alongside the miracle-working Antichrist comes another figure that cheerleads the worship of the man of sin.

Then I saw another beast coming up from the earth. He had two horns like a lamb, but was speaking like a dragon [definite description of a wolf in sheep's clothing!]. *He exercised all the ruling authority of the first beast on his behalf, and made the earth and those who inhabit it worship the first beast, the one whose lethal wound had been healed. He performed momentous signs, even making fire come down from heaven in front of people* (Rev 13:11-13, NET).

This wolf in sheep's clothing, who has the power to cause fire to come down from heaven, is later identified as the False Prophet. This False Prophet, whose ecclesiastical office is already evident on the earth today, is very much like Simon the Sorcerer in that the world is already bewitched into believing that he is the very representative of God on earth. And, if you can accept this, the False Prophet will be the last Pope. But both the Beast and the False Prophet will suffer the same fate:

*And the **beast was taken, and with him the false prophet that wrought miracles before him**, with which he deceived them that had received the mark of the beast, and them that worshipped his image. These both were cast alive into a lake of fire burning with brimstone* (Rev 19:20).

And yet, for all of Satan's miracles, his real intentions is the deceive God's elect.

For false messiahs and false prophets will appear and perform great signs and wonders to deceive, if possible, even the elect (Mt 24:24, NIV).

Hence the repeated warning from the word of God is for Christians to not be deceived!

THE BLASPHEMOUS MARK

Offspring of vipers! How can you, being evil, speak good things? For out of the abundance of the heart the mouth speaks (Mt 12:34, MKJV).

And speak he does! For out of his mouth, the Antichrist speaks *great things* and *great words* (Dan 7:8, 11, 20); he *blasphemes God, His Name, His tabernacle, and them that dwell in heaven* (Rev 13:6).

The Antichrist is so characteristically blasphemous that God emblazons the seven heads of the Antichrist beast with the name *Blasphemy* (Rev 13:1).

One can commit *blasphemy* in several ways. It can be done by speaking against God or anything holy and sacred (as when the Jews criticized the things of God that Paul spoke about in Acts 13:45). Blasphemy can also be done when someone declares himself to be God (as when the High Priests thought Jesus was blaspheming when He declared that He was the Son of God, Jn 10:33, Mk 14:61-64). It can also be done when one attributes the power of God to Satan. This is the blasphemy of the Holy Spirit, which cannot be forgiven (Mk 3:22, 28-29).

Therefore, the Antichrist is guilty of blasphemy on several levels. In fact, it is Satan's true feelings that are coming out of the mouth of the Antichrist, for blasphemy has been a part of Satan since he first rebelled as Lucifer.

> *How art thou fallen from heaven, O Lucifer, son of the morning! how art thou cut down to the ground, which didst weaken the nations!* **For thou hast said in thine heart, I will ascend into heaven, I will exalt my throne above the stars of God: I will sit also upon the mount of the congregation, in the sides of the north: I will ascend above the heights of the clouds; I will be like the most High.** *Yet thou shalt be brought down to hell, to the sides of the pit* (Isa 14:12-15).

I will be like the most High! And, so, the devil-incarnated Antichrist pawns himself off as god to a deceived world.

Other areas in which Antichrist will blaspheme include denials that Jesus is the Son of God (1 Jn 2:22), who came in the flesh to die for the sins of mankind (1 Jn 4:3).

Interestingly, the Apostle Paul makes a startling confession when recalling his actions as a blasphemous persecutor of saints (1 Timothy 1:13). He was not just content to persecute them, but he reveled in causing the saints to blaspheme as well.

> *And I punished them often in every synagogue;* **I compelled them to blaspheme** (Acts 26:11, MKJV).

OTHER MARKS OF THE BEAST

In this same way, and with that same mindset, the Antichrist will try to cause everyone, saint and sinner alike, to blaspheme as well. That's what the mark of the beast is all about.

> *And he causeth all, both small and great, rich and poor, free and bond,* **to receive a mark in their right hand, or in their foreheads:** *And that no man might buy or sell, save he that had the mark, or the name of the beast, or the number of his name* (Rev 13:16-17).

The *he* referred to here is the False Prophet, who acts as the Antichrist's chief supporter. **Therefore, it is the False Prophet, not the Antichrist, who imposes this blasphemous mark on all mankind!**

Read from Revelation 13:11 onward and you'll see that it is the False Prophet, using his self-appointed moral authority, who does the following things:

- performs great miracles
- affirms the Antichrist as god
- compels the world to worship Antichrist as god (citing his "resurrection")
- commands the building of an "image to the beast"
- compels the world to worship this image
- and takes control of the world's economy by compelling all to receive this mark

This mark, probably a microchip that is inserted inside man's skin, is already in use in many parts of the world today – *in order to get the world accustomed to them now!*

Pets are being equipped with microchips in case they get lost. The U.S. Federal Drug Administration is pushing a plan to use embedded chips on patients in order to preserve one's medical history. Some are even considering imposing a fertility chip to control the population. And one company in Sweden has begun a practice of implanting their employees with microchips for the mundane uses of making copies at the printer, opening security doors and even paying for their lunches.

The irony is that many the world over will think this is a major advancement to mankind and will see no harm in allowing the chip to be implanted.

However, this implantation will be a *blasphemous mark* of one's obedience to the beast power that arises. **We would strongly advise one and all not to receive the mark, no matter how logical it all sounds.** We've seen many times already that the world's despots push through their agenda with nice-sounding trappings of progress and solutions, only to snare their prey.

They may even promote it as a way to preserve cyber security and to prevent identity theft, but it is a demonic, blasphemous injection upon mankind from which there's no escape.

> *And the first* [destroying angel] *went, and poured out his vial upon the earth; and* **there fell a noisome and grievous sore upon the men which had the mark of the beast, and upon them which worshipped his image** (Rev 16:2)

> *And the third angel followed them, saying with a loud voice,* **If any man worship the beast and his image, and receive his mark in his forehead, or in his hand, The same shall drink of the wine of the wrath of God, which is poured out without mixture into the cup of his indignation; and he shall be tormented with fire and brimstone in the presence of the holy angels, and in the presence of the Lamb: And the smoke of their torment ascendeth up for ever and ever: and they have no rest day nor night, who worship the beast and his**

image, and whosoever receiveth the mark of his name (Rev 14:9-11).

As the first verse shows, there is an equivalency between those who receive this mark and those who worship his image. The mark represents submission to Satan and rejection of God. The Antichrist's whole system is associated with the term *blasphemy* and the False Prophet promotes the worship of the *Blasphemer!*

In the second verse, notice the eternal punishment of those who receive the mark which, judging by their punishment, is equivalent to blaspheming the Holy Spirit (Mt 12:31).

Well said was Jesus' statement, in the very context of His return and the rapture:

> *And as it was in the days of Noe, so shall it be also in the days of the Son of man. They did eat, they drank, they married wives, they were given in marriage, until the day that Noe entered into the ark, and the flood came, and destroyed them all. Likewise also as it was in the days of Lot; they did eat, they drank, they bought, they sold, they planted, they builded; But the same day that Lot went out of Sodom it rained fire and brimstone from heaven, and destroyed them all. Even thus shall it be in the day when the Son of man is revealed. In that day, he which shall be upon the housetop, and his stuff in the house, let him not come down to take it away: and he that is in the field, let him likewise not return back. Remember Lot's wife.* ***Whosoever shall seek to save his life shall lose it; and whosoever shall lose his life shall preserve it.*** *I tell you, in that night there shall be two men in one bed; the one shall be taken, and the other shall be left. Two women shall be grinding together; the one shall be taken, and the other left. Two men shall be in the field; the one shall be taken, and the other left* (Lk 17:26-36).

131

ESCAPE THE COMING ANTICHRIST

Seeking to save your physical life in the Great Tribulation, *by receiving the mark (!),* **will only get you a possible extension of a few more years in this physical life, but then you'll receive the wrath of God and loss of eternal life.** Whoever loses his physical life at the hands of Antichrist and/or endures to the end will be saved and have eternal life (Mt 24:13).

The choice to either receive or reject the mark will result in eternal consequences. This is why the scripture can then say this:

> *He that is unjust, let him be unjust still: and he which is filthy, let him be filthy still: and he that is righteous, let him be righteous still: and he that is holy, let him be holy still* (Rev 22:11).

At this point, there is no more turning back!

One chapter in the book of Luke encourages Christians, should they be caught and compelled to take the mark, to maintain their faithful resolve against the Antichrist forces. In essence, the Lord is preparing His people that no matter what it looks like during the tribulation, no matter the difficulties, no matter the hardship, they are valued in the sight of God and they must stand true to God's word.

> *And I say unto you my friends,* **Be not afraid of them that kill the body, and after that have no more that they can do. But I will forewarn you whom ye shall fear: Fear him, which after he hath killed hath power to cast into hell; yea, I say unto you, Fear him.** *Are not five sparrows sold for two farthings, and not one of them is forgotten before God? But even the very hairs of your head are all numbered. Fear not therefore:* **ye are of more value than many sparrows** *(Lk 12:4-7).*

The Antichrist forces will compel Christians to deny the Godhead, with the ultimate objective of committing blasphemy. But Christians are to reject their coercive tactics and confess the Lord Jesus.

> *Also I say unto you, Whosoever shall confess me before men, him shall the Son of man also confess before the angels of God: But he that denieth me before men shall be denied before the angels of God.* ***And whosoever shall speak a word against the Son of man, it shall be forgiven him: but unto him that blasphemeth against the Holy Ghost it shall not be forgiven*** (Lk 12:8-10).

To the Christian who stands tall, though frightened, will the Holy Spirit give inspiration on how to respond.

> *And when they bring you unto the synagogues, and unto magistrates, and powers, take ye no thought how or what thing ye shall answer, or what ye shall say:* ***For the Holy Ghost shall teach you in the same hour what ye ought to say*** (Lk 12:11-12).

If you're wondering why we haven't seen these scriptures in this light before, it's because we've been programmed to believe that Christians aren't even going to be here on the earth at that time, and so we miss out on these clues. We also don't see how these difficult scriptures pertain to us now, so we casually disregard them.

Yet Jesus tells us these things beforehand, and this volume is presenting this point of view so that Christians don't get easily offended and disillusioned in the face of tribulation, hardship and death.

> *If the world hate you, ye know that it hated me before it hated you. If ye were of the world, the world would love his own: but because ye are not of*

the world, but I have chosen you out of the world, therefore the world hateth you. Remember the word that I said unto you, The servant is not greater than his lord. **If they have persecuted me, they will also persecute you;** *if they have kept my saying, they will keep yours also. But all these things will they do unto you for my name's sake, because they know not him that sent me. If I had not come and spoken unto them, they had not had sin: but now they have no cloke for their sin. He that hateth me hateth my Father also. If I had not done among them the works which none other man did, they had not had sin: but now have they both seen and hated both me and my Father. But this cometh to pass, that the word might be fulfilled that is written in their law, They hated me without a cause...***These things have I spoken unto you, that ye should not be offended.*** They shall put you out of the synagogues: yea, **the time cometh, that whosoever killeth you will think that he doeth God service.** And these things will they do unto you, because they have not known the Father, nor me. **But these things have I told you, that when the time shall come, ye may remember that I told you of them** (Jn 15:18-25, 16:1-4).

Stand tall, Christian! You were born at this time for a reason. And God will supply all of our needs to fulfill the work He has given us to do. He won't fail us, so long as we don't fail ourselves and retreat.

Jesus, like a fearless General, is confiding to His troops the difficulties of the days ahead. He's preparing them to build a strong resolve to maintain the faith, despite the opposition. He's preparing them to never give up, and to go all the way. He's preparing them to wage war and to win the battles ahead – and *faith* is how battles are won! He is telling His people that our greatest days of victory are just ahead.

Do not shrink back, do not lose faith.

The two primary emotions in the last days will be either fear and faith. Soldier in the army of God, which shall we exhibit?

We can be encouraged, as we'll see in a later chapter, how that God will be with us during these extraordinarily tough times in order to help us endure to the end.

Yet God promises salvation, celebration and eternal rewards for His children who reject the mark of the beast.

> *And I saw as it were a sea of glass mingled with fire: and* **them that had gotten the victory over the beast, and over his image, and over his mark, and over the number of his name, stand on the sea of glass, having the harps of God.** *And they sing the song of Moses the servant of God, and the song of the Lamb, saying, Great and marvellous are thy works, Lord God Almighty; just and true are thy ways, thou King of saints. Who shall not fear thee, O Lord, and glorify thy name? for thou only art holy: for all nations shall come and worship before thee; for thy judgments are made manifest* (Rev 15:2-4);

> *And I saw thrones, and they sat upon them, and judgment was given unto them: and I saw the* **souls of them that were beheaded for the witness of Jesus, and for the word of God, and which had not worshipped the beast, neither his image, neither had received his mark upon their foreheads, or in their hands; and they lived and reigned with Christ a thousand years** (Rev 20:4).

The Antichrist will use his mouth to speak great pompous words of blasphemy against the Lord and against everything sacred. When the Lord returns, interestingly enough, the Lord will use His own mouth to destroy the wicked one.

> *And then shall that Wicked be revealed,* **whom the Lord shall consume with the spirit of his mouth,**

and shall destroy with the brightness of his coming
(2 Thess 2:8).

Let's now move onto other characteristics of the beast.

IS HE A GAY MUSLIM?

Much has been said lately, by prominent Christians, that the
Antichrist is possibly gay and possibly Muslim. Let's dispel
of those two notions right now. The concept that he may be
homosexual comes from this verse, speaking of the
Antichrist:

> *Neither shall he regard the God of his fathers, **nor the
> desire of women,** nor regard any god: for he shall
> magnify himself above all* (Dan 11:37).

Is it really saying that Antichrist is not attracted to
women? Let's start breaking down this verse. The first
clause says, *neither shall he regard the God of his fathers.*
That phrase, *the God of his fathers* is consistently used in
scripture to denote the God of Abraham, Isaac and Jacob, as
in Exodus 3:15. The word *God* is actually translated from
the Hebrew word for *Elohim,* which is used over 2,000 times
in the Bible, which means it's talking about the God of the
Bible.

When we realize that Antichrist is Jewish, this verse
makes quite a bit of sense. He will reject the God of his
fathers!

If we look at the phrase as a whole, we realize that there
are three clauses in it. The first and third clause both refer to
Antichrist's rejection of other gods. But that middle verse,
nor the desire of women, doesn't seem to fit in this
paragraph. Or does it? We should know by now that God
doesn't normally inject unrelated clauses within a thought.
Let's explore this a bit more. The NIV translates it this way:

He will show no regard for the gods of his ancestors
or for the one desired by women, *nor will he regard
any god, but will exalt himself above them all* (Dan
11:37, NIV).

We see a more definite pattern here. The entire thought
for this passage is that Antichrist exalts himself above all
other gods. The second clause doesn't seem to be so out of
place now. But what is the meaning of *the one desired by
women?*

Eschatology writer John F. Walvoord, author of the
"Prophecy Knowledge Handbook," offers this explanation for
that mysterious phrase.

"From the Jewish perspective, *the desire of
women* was to fulfill the promise to Eve of a
coming Redeemer to be born of a woman (i.e.,
the promise of Genesis 3:15). Undoubtedly,
many Jewish women hoped that one of their sons
would fulfill this prophecy. Accordingly, the one
desired by women, is the Messiah of Israel"
(page 272).

Seeing it from that perspective, we can understand the
entire verse as a whole, i.e., "Antichrist will exalt himself
above the God of Abraham, Isaac and Jacob, above the
promised Messiah, and above all other gods!"

That makes sense. That should settle the matter about
whether this scripture says he's gay or not.

Now we move onto a very controversial topic, actually a
very misguided theory, made popular by several well-
meaning ministers on TV and YouTube.

It seems that all throughout the ages, biblical prophecies
have been interpreted to reflect the then current geopolitical
realities. Therefore it's no great stretch of the imagination that
with the rise of Islamic terrorism, some have suggested that

the Antichrist *must* be Islamic. And why not? Islam is the chief antagonist against the Jewish state today. And, with the growing number of Christian and Jewish casualties at the hands of Islamic terrorists worldwide, it's become a popular conception among many groups.

To further support this claim, Walid Shoebat, the Muslim-turned-Christian, set social media ablaze with his controversial theory that the book of Revelation contains one portion written in Arabic! Let's look first at the scripture:

> *And he causeth all, both small and great, rich and poor, free and bond, to receive a mark in their right hand, or in their foreheads: And that no man might buy or sell, save he that had the mark, or the name of the beast, or the number of his name.* **Here is wisdom. Let him that hath understanding count the number of the beast: for it is the number of a man; and his number is Six hundred threescore and six** (Rev 13:16-18).

He says, in essence, that the Greek phase for 666, which is the mark of the beast, isn't actually Greek at all, but *Arabic*. That's interesting, since John wrote the book of Revelation in the first century AD and the Arabic language hadn't come into existence until the sixth century AD!

Shoebat alleges that the Greek numbers Chi Xi Stigma (666) translated by John are *not* the number 666 at all, but an Arabic phrase, the *bismillah*, meaning *in the name of Allah.*

Below is the number 666 in the lower case Greek, as found in Shoebat's favorite text, the Codex Vaticanus.

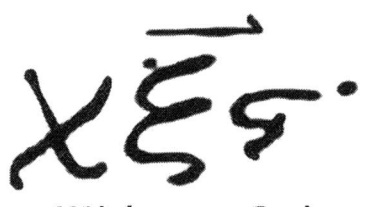

666 in lower case Greek

Below is the Arabic depiction of *in the name of Allah,* which is presented as proof by those who support Shoebat's view.

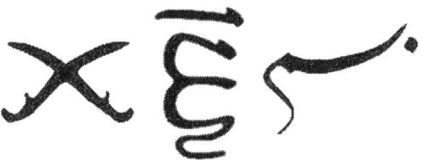

In the name of Allah in Arabic

They look remarkably alike, don't they? But this isn't totally accurate. A more accurate, side-by-side rendering of the two images would be this one:

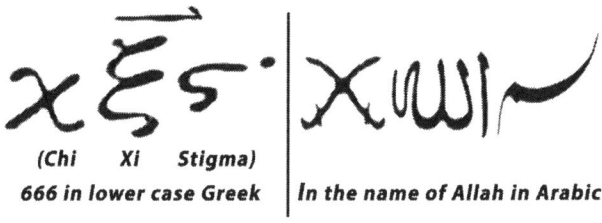

(Chi   Xi   Stigma)
666 in lower case Greek | *In the name of Allah in Arabic*

You will notice that defenders of Shoebat's theory have to *reverse* the *Xi* letter and *invert* it 90 degrees to make it resemble the Arabic phrase. Does that sound biblically accurate? Would John, who was given the revelation, suddenly depart from the Greek in order to begin writing in a language that hasn't even originated yet? I can see some thinking, "Yes, God can do that. God can do anything." Okay then, would God also expect you to know to invert the middle letter sideways and then flip it backwards? Because that's what these defenders of this position have to do in order to make us believe that John wrote in Arabic.

To be fair, it doesn't look so similar now, does it?

Furthermore, the Chi Xi Stigma letters are *all in the lower case Greek!* John did not write in lower case Greek (!), as it would not come into existence until hundreds of years later.

But understand this: the Codex Vaticanus, one of the oldest extant manuscripts of the Greek Bible (Old and New Testaments), which Shoebat relies upon so heavily *never contained the book of Revelation.*

The book of Revelation, and other missing books, were added to the Codex Vaticanus hundreds of years later. "These missing leaves were supplemented by a 15th-century minuscule hand," which is the term for the lower case Greek (Source: Wikipedia page on the Codex Vaticanus).

That means that the lower case Greek was not how John the Apostle wrote Chi Xi Stigma.

When you refer to an earlier version of the Bible, you'll notice that the 666 is rendered in the classical Greek and looks nothing like the Arabic now.

This is 666 as seen in the earliest text available: the Chester Beatty Biblical Papyri P47, dated the third century AD.

There is a line going across the top of the letters to help readers differentiate between letters and numbers, because all Greek letters had a numerical value. When a number was intended, a line was drawn above it.

666 in original Classical Greek

Hence, we see the original Greek supports a number and not an Arabic phrase.

We therefore reject the notion that the mark of the beast is going to be an Islamic branding of *in the name of Allah*, no matter how popular a concept it becomes. We have shown throughout this volume that the Antichrist, in order to counterfeit the true Messiah, will be Jewish and will try to mimic Jesus in every way. No one will accept a Muslim Antichrist. No Jewish person would follow a Muslim Antichrist. No Christian would be fooled by a Muslim Antichrist. If a Muslim Antichrist ever appeared, it would immediately be spotted as demonic by everyone!

But suppose that the Antichrist comes in as a mighty Jewish war hero, who vanquishes Israel's enemies and brings retribution to the Arab terrorist nations that have threatened Israel for so long? You can bet that both the Jewish and Christian populations will put their support right behind the Antichrist!

That's why Jesus warns us not to be deceived!

And we shouldn't be deceived about the mark of the beast, either. We still maintain it is going to be a microchip that will be implanted into one's skin, by which they can track you, monitor your purchases, catalog your medical history, and cause you to reject God.

It will seem so high-tech and so beneficial to mankind, and yet its claws are filled with poison from hell.

We have been attempting in this volume to lay out a firm timeline for the end days and the return of Jesus Christ, so that His people will not be caught off guard or deceived by anything.

We have tried to encourage the reader that even though the Church will go through the Great Tribulation, God will still be able to protect His people (more on that in later chapters).

We have seen that the Antichrist will be Jewish, and not Islamic, as many are now claiming. We have shown how deceptive the end times are going to be for the many.

We have tried to bring clarity about the timing of the rapture and to correct mindsets that are misinformed.

Now let's take a look at that much misunderstood *Mystery Babylon.*

9
SURPRISE! MYSTERY BABYLON
IS JERUSALEM

At the time when the World Trade Center's Twin Towers collapsed, I heard a minister declare that this was a fulfillment of this scripture: "Babylon is fallen, is fallen!" Apparently, the double adjective referred to the two buildings of America's financial system.

One of the "go-to" biblical supplementary books in my youth was "Babylon Mystery Religion." This book attempted to prove that Babylon was the Roman Catholic Church.

It seems that with every end-time, biblical symbolism, there are myriad interpretations to befuddle the mind. And while there may be elements of Babylon all throughout our corrupted systems, and all throughout the ages, we need to accept the correct biblical definition for Revelation's Mystery Babylon, the one associated with the Antichrist.

It shouldn't surprise anyone that if the Antichrist isn't on the world's scene yet, neither is Mystery Babylon – for the two are inseparable and neither can function without the other.

Our continued inability to fully understand biblical symbolisms has caused us no end of speculation, which always leads us to dead ends and wrong conclusions.

The whole premise of this chapter is to prove that Mystery Babylon is not anything like what we've been taught, but is something we hold sacred – the city of Jerusalem. That sounds far fetched to many, and even blasphemous to some. Yet Jerusalem is not *yet* Mystery Babylon. It only becomes Mystery Babylon when it rides the Antichrist beast, which is still some undetermined time in the future.

You might want to review Revelation chapters 17 and 18 to get an overview of Mystery Babylon, which is famously depicted in Revelation 17:5 as "MYSTERY, BABYLON THE GREAT, THE MOTHER OF HARLOTS AND ABOMINATIONS OF THE EARTH."

This harlot woman is also depicted in Revelation 17:3 as riding the Antichrist beast of Revelation 13, the one with seven heads and ten horns (which we've already discussed). She is suddenly enjoying a lucrative association with the Antichrist. And while it might seem that this woman is *controlling* the beast, it's more a depiction of the woman going along for the ride and enriching herself tremendously.

Before we proceed, let's first review.

The Antichrist is Jewish, and appears on the world's scene when he affirms a covenant to reinstitute Temple worship in Jerusalem. This act provokes neighboring Arab nations, and he wages successful military campaigns routing Israel's enemies. He finally enters the newly constructed Temple and demands the world's worship. Notice:

And he shall plant the tabernacles of his palace between the seas in the glorious holy mountain (Dan 11:45).

Between the seas is a metaphor for between the Dead and Mediterranean Seas. The *glorious holy mountain* can be none other than Jerusalem, as in Zechariah 8:3: *Thus says the LORD: I have returned to Zion and will dwell in the midst of*

Jerusalem, and Jerusalem shall be called the faithful city, and the mountain of the LORD of hosts, the holy mountain, [English Standard Version, see also Joel 3:17].

He plants himself, i.e., he establishes his headquarters there in Jerusalem – not Rome, not Mecca, not New York City, or anywhere else! Now with that background, let's take a fresh look at an age-old dilemma. Let's be open to a mind shift of sorts and accept where the scriptures and the Holy Spirit lead us.

MYSTERY BABYLON IS A GREAT CITY

Let's go over some of the many characteristics of Mystery Babylon. The first mention of Babylon, in the book of Revelation, tells us that it is a *great city*.

> *And there followed another angel, saying, **Babylon** is fallen, is fallen, **that great city**…*(Rev 14:8).

Here's a heads-up: every time Revelation mentions the word *city*, it's referring to either the future Jerusalem from where the Antichrist rules the world, or to the far distant *future* Jerusalem, called the *new* Jerusalem, from where God the Father establishes His rule on the earth. *Revelation does not use that word to denote any other city.*

Though it isn't now, Jerusalem will soon become that *great city*, the epicenter of end-time events, once Antichrist establishes his rule there.

Bible students are aware of a foundational principle in bible study. It's called the "law of first mention," which is described this way by Gotquestions.org: "The law of first mention says that, to understand a particular word or doctrine, **we must find the first place in scripture that word or doctrine is revealed and study that passage.** The reasoning is that the Bible's first mention of a concept is the simplest and clearest presentation; doctrines are then more fully developed on that foundation. **So, to fully understand an important and complex theological concept, Bible students are advised to start with its 'first mention.'"** [Ref: www.gotquestions.org/law-of-first-mention.html.]

Notice that in the book of Revelation, the very first mention of the term *great city*, God gives us the identity of Mystery Babylon. Speaking of the two witnesses, who will prophecy during the Great Tribulation, it says:

> *And their dead bodies shall lie in the street of the* ***great city, which spiritually is called Sodom and Egypt, where also our Lord was crucified*** (Rev 11:8).

Our Lord was crucified in Jerusalem, therefore each time the term *great city* is referred to in the following verses, it is talking about Jerusalem! [Rev 11:8; 14:8; 16:19; 17:18; 18:10; 18:16; 18:18; 18:19; 18:21.]

A CITY THAT MARTYRS GOD'S PEOPLE

> *And I saw the woman* [the harlot] ***drunken with the blood of the saints, and with the blood of the martyrs of Jesus:*** *and when I saw her, I wondered with great admiration* (Rev 17:6)

> *And* ***in her was found the blood of prophets, and of saints,*** *and of all that were slain upon the earth* (Rev 18:24).

It shouldn't shock anyone that Jerusalem is depicted this way. Jerusalem has a legacy of killing the prophets. Jesus said, *Oh Jerusalem, Jerusalem, you that kill the prophets, and stone them that are sent to you* (Mt 23:37). And, in another place, Jesus said, *for it cannot be that a prophet perishes outside of Jerusalem* (Lk 13:33). The New Living Translation makes the point more clearly this way: *For it wouldn't do for a prophet of God to be killed except in Jerusalem!*

It is no great surprise, therefore, that when the disciples asked Jesus about the last days, He warned them that as soon as the Antichrist demands worship as god that they should flee *Jerusalem* to avoid persecution (Mt 24:15-21).

Whatever Jerusalem's sins were in the past, they will pale in comparison when the woman rides the beast. This woman will be *drunken with the blood of saints and martyrs of Jesus*, for she is a harlot.

MOTHER OF HARLOTS

It is this appellation, more than any other, that many Bible teachers use as basis for identifying Mystery Babylon as Rome or the Roman Catholic Church. Using the biblical analogy that a woman denotes a church, they refer to the following verse to conclude that the Catholic Church is the *mother* of all apostate churches:

> *And upon her forehead was a name written, MYSTERY, BABYLON THE GREAT, THE MOTHER OF HARLOTS AND ABOMINATIONS OF THE EARTH* (Rev 17:5).

But notice the scripture does not use the word *all*, as in *all* apostate churches, although the New Living Translation inserts an *all*, i.e., *Mother of All Prostitutes and Obscenities in the World.* However, we believe, this is in keeping with the modern embrace of the interpretation.

The original Greek does not imply *all*. It simply describes her as a mother of harlots. Like mother, like daughters; like city, like citizens – they both act abominably.

The concept of Jerusalem depicted as a harlot is nothing new. The scriptures are replete with references wherein the Lord calls Jerusalem a harlot. The prophetic first chapter of

Isaiah is addressed to "Judah and Jerusalem" (Isa 1:1), and then in the Lord's list of grievances, it says this:

> **How is the faithful city become an harlot!** *it was full of judgment; righteousness lodged in it;* **but now murderers** (Isa 1:21).

The reader is encouraged to go through the first few chapters of Jeremiah and see how closely related Mystery Babylon is with Jerusalem, for it is surely true that the Bible interprets the Bible. For brevity's sake, we shall only list the words and phrases that make our point:

- *Go and cry in the ears of* **Jerusalem** (Jer 2:2)
- *your own* **sword** *hath devoured your* **prophets** (2:30)
- *thou hast polluted the land with thy* **whoredoms** *and with thy wickedness* (3:2)
- *thou hadst a* **whore's forehead** (3:3)
- *backsliding Israel committed adultery…yet her treacherous sister Judah feared not, but went and* **played the harlot also** (3:8)
- *through the lightness of her* **whoredom,** *that she defiled the land, and* **committed adultery** *with stones and with stocks* (3:9)
- *I am* **married** *unto you* (3:14)
- *if thou wilt put away thine* **abominations** *out of my sight* (4:1)

Ezekiel, too, one of the major prophets of the Old Testament, takes Jerusalem to task for her whoredom. Again, for brevity's sake, we'll list the highlights in Ezekiel 16.

- *Again the Word of Jehovah came to me, saying, Son of man,* **cause Jerusalem to know her abominations** (Ezek 16:1-2, MKJV throughout)

- *But you ... **played the harlot** because of your name, and poured out **your fornications** on all who passed by* (16:15)
- *And in all your hateful deeds and your **fornications*** (16:22)
- *You have also **whored with the Egyptians** ... and have multiplied your fornications to provoke Me to anger* (16:26)
- *You have **whored with the Assyrians** ... yea, you whored and yet you were not satisfied* (16:28)
- *your **whoredom is idolatry*** (16:29)
- *an overbearing **harlot*** (16:30)
- *Like the **adulterous wife**, instead of her husband, she takes strangers* (16:32)
- *They give a gift to all **harlots**, but you give your gifts to all your lovers, and bribe them to come to you from all around, for your fornication* (16:33)
- *And in you was the opposite from those women in **your fornications**, since no one whores after you, and in your giving wages, and hire is not given to you* (16:34)
- *Therefore, O **harlot**, hear the Word of Jehovah* (16:35)
- *behold, therefore I will **gather all your lovers**, with whom you have been pleased, even all whom you loved, with all whom you have hated; I will even gather them against you from all around, and will **uncover your nakedness to them**, and they will see all your nakedness* (16:37)

And we can go on, but we'll forbear. Here we see many similarities between Mystery Babylon and Jerusalem. And as

Revelation confirms the word in Ezekiel, Jerusalem will be judged as her lovers view her nakedness and destruction (Rev 17:16; 18:3; 18:9).

But consider how great is Jerusalem's harlotry. The real Messiah had already come and was rejected by Judah. Now, in riding the beast, Jerusalem causes the world to submit to her lover, the Antichrist. Revelation 14:8 says, the harlot *made all nations drink the wine of the passion of her sexual immorality* (ESV).

Many who sense that the *mother of harlots* aspect has a religious connotation are not mistaken. But people forget that by worshipping the Antichrist as God, this becomes a new false religion, unlike anything the world has seen before. It will be embraced as a new, but false, religious paradigm that will be accepted by the world.

Jerusalem will embrace this lover as god and will promote him to the kings of the earth. The False Prophet, representing the leader of the Catholic Church, will also submit his religion to this new idolatrous concept that Antichrist is God. The Muslim world will also accept Antichrist as their Mahdi, as he will fulfill their own eschatological prophecies.

How true is the word that says, *Satan has deceived the whole world* (Rev 12:9).

SHE LIVED DELICIOUSLY

As we've said before, Mystery Babylon knows how to ride the beast to her own gratification. When the scriptures say that "she lived deliciously" (Rev 18:7), it means that she lived lavishly and luxuriously.

She milked it for all it was worth.

And it was worth plenty. Remember that once the world is subjected to a global economy from which there is no escape, and once the world is compelled to accept the mark of the beast, which regulates purchases and sales, who do you think stands to profit from this global currency extortion?

Why of course, the Antichrist and his headquarters, Jerusalem, stand to profit. And look at how luxuriously Mystery Babylon is described.

> *And the woman was arrayed in purple and scarlet. And she was gilded with gold and precious stones and pearls, having a golden cup in her hand full of abominations and filthiness of her fornication* (Rev 17:4).

An interesting bible study, to further identify Mystery Babylon as Jerusalem, is to do a comparison study between the items traded by the merchants in Revelation 18 with the items needed for the reinstitution of Temple worship in Jerusalem. Revelation 18:11-13 identifies the following items the merchants are trading, while Old Testament passages identify these same items as crucial to temple worship:

- Gold, silver and precious stones (1 Chr 29:1-3)
- Fine linen, purple and scarlet (Ex 36:8)
- Precious wood, brass, iron and marble (1 Chr 29:1-3)
- Cinnamon, odors and ointments (Ex 30:22-26);
- Frankincense, wine, oil and fine flour (1 Chr 9:29)
- Wheat, beasts and sheep (Ezra 6:9)

Not only has Jerusalem grown in wealth, but so have her lovers, the kings and merchants of the earth. There is plenty of wealth to go around.

> *...the merchants of the earth are waxed rich through the abundance of her delicacies ... And the kings of the earth, who have committed fornication and lived deliciously with her ...* (Rev 18:3, 9).

We shall see, in the next few sections, how the kings of the earth actually turn on Jerusalem. But let us first present evidence that Mystery Babylon is not Rome or the Catholic Church.

PETER IN BABYLON

Your sister church here in Babylon sends you greetings, and so does my son Mark (1 Pet 5:13).

Peter the Apostle identifies the very place from where he wrote the first of his epistles – *Babylon!* Historically, there has been no end of arguments over whether Peter was in the literal Babylon, Rome or Jerusalem.

So intent is the Roman Catholic Church to prove that Peter was the first pope that they accept this rather derogatory appellation in order to try to prove that Peter was in Rome.

And there are countless commentaries that would support that claim, but they do so with very little evidence. It would appear that long before "fake news" became apparent in the American liberal news media, we had "fake history" long before that.

There is no proof that Peter ever set foot in Rome, despite the fact that the entire history of the Catholic Church revolves around this false foundation.

We've alluded already to Simon the Sorcerer of Acts 8 and we maintain that it was he (*who used sorcery, and bewitched the people of Samaria, giving out that himself was some great one,* Acts 8:9) who had more of the characteristics of the papacy than he did to Peter.

It's interesting to note that in the next few verses Peter confronts this Simon, who desired the gifts of God to promote himself, and Peter commands him to repent of wanting to merchandize the anointing of God (Acts 8:18-23).

There are other resources that document the errors in Catholic Church teachings, so we will not dwell on them here, save for this one scripture the Catholic Church bases its whole existence on:

> *And I say also unto thee, That thou art Peter (Petros), and upon this rock (petra) I will build my church; and the gates of hell shall not prevail against it* (Mt 16:18).

The Catholic Church revels in the thought that Jesus was saying that the Church was going to be built on Peter. Is that what it says? Does that sound true? Isn't *Jesus* the foundation of the Church? Let's look at the entire context and see.

> *[Jesus] saith unto them, But whom say ye that I am? And Simon Peter answered and said, Thou art the Christ, the Son of the living God.* And Jesus answered and said unto him, *Blessed art thou, Simon Barjona: for flesh and blood hath not revealed it unto thee, but my Father which is in heaven. And I say also unto thee, That thou art Peter, and upon this rock I will build my church;* and the gates of hell shall not prevail against it (Mt 16:15-18).

Jesus was affirming that this knowledge that Jesus is the Son of God is the foundation of the Church! Jesus used a play on words, when he said, "you are Petros, (small rock) but upon *this* petra (large boulder) I will build my Church." That *large boulder* is the acknowledgment that Jesus is the Son of God.

No one can biblically make the claim that Peter overrides Jesus in importance. Where is the biblical support that Jesus, the Son of God, would give a human being the authority to rule the Church? Do we pray to Jesus or to Peter? Does spiritual knowledge come from Jesus or from the Papacy?

Those last two statements probably open up a theological can of worms for the Catholic Church because the Papacy has always promoted the teaching of praying to saints and has always prided itself as being able to usurp scripture. Yet the Word says that Jesus is the only mediator between man and God (1 Tim 2:5), that man should live by every word that proceeds from the mouth of God (Mt 4:4), and that Jesus is the head of the Church (Col 1:18).

But getting back to Peter in Babylon, we know through scripture that Peter was the Apostle over the Jerusalem congregation during the early days of the Church (Acts 1-12). Conversely, there are no scriptural references saying that Peter was an Apostle over Rome or even ministered there. If God had wanted us to know that Peter was the first Pope, He would have clearly shown us that.

Furthermore, one who would know is the Apostle Paul. He was twice imprisoned in Rome, from where he wrote many of his epistles: Ephesians, Philippians, Colossians and Philemon. And in none of his writings does he ever mention that the Apostle Peter was present in that city. In fact, even when writing the book to the Romans, circa 58 AD, supposedly 16 years after Peter started the Church there, Paul doesn't mention Peter at all. And in the last chapter of Romans, Paul, writing from Corinth, sends salutations to 27 individual saints and leaders to the church at Rome, and Peter is not mentioned at all.

What an oversight! Imagine the one who supposedly started the church in Rome is never acknowledged as such anywhere in scripture.

Yet Peter, having read the major and minor prophetic books of the Old Testament, would have understood Babylon as being Jerusalem and not Rome anyway. And, speaking of the Old Testament, let's move on now to a profoundly illuminating passage of scripture that deals specifically with Babylon's King and the power behind him.

154

KING OF BABYLON

The following scriptures, to my knowledge, haven't been used as a reference to the Antichrist before, but it seems quite apparent now in light of the teachings in this book. Up till now, the scriptures seemed to be referring to the overthrow of the ancient King of Babylon by God. But quite often there is a duality application in scripture, in that certain prophetic scriptures have more than one meaning and involve more than one timeframe.

"The Elijah to come," for instance, had a dual application. The first application had already been fulfilled, in part, by John the Baptist. Yet another and, in fact, the more definitive application of the scripture is yet to be fulfilled [compare Mal 4:5; Lk 1:17; Mt 17:10-13; Rev 11:3].

The following scripture begins talking about the judgment of the King of Babylon and then it morphs into a condemnation of the spirit operating behind the King of Babylon – Lucifer (or Satan)!

And, of course, that's true! The King of Babylon (Antichrist) receives all power from Satan anyway, and worship to Antichrist is worship to Satan (Rev 13:4).

We should realize that the Antichrist's entire existence is to replicate in human form the character, aspirations and power of Satan himself. Both revel in self-glory, control and oppression of the world, and both will be defeated, destroyed and removed by Jesus.

Read this and see if you come away from this passage understanding it in a new way.

*In that wonderful day when the LORD gives his people rest from sorrow and fear, from slavery and chains, **you will taunt the king of Babylon. You will say, "The mighty man has been destroyed. Yes, your insolence is ended.***

For the LORD has crushed your wicked power and broken your evil rule. You struck the people with endless blows of rage and held the nations in your angry grip with unrelenting tyranny.

But finally the earth is at rest and quiet. Now it can sing again! Even the trees of the forest— the cypress trees and the cedars of Lebanon— sing out this joyous song: 'Since you have been cut down, no one will come now to cut us down!'

"In the place of the dead [hades, sheol] there is excitement over your arrival. The spirits of world leaders and mighty kings long dead stand up to see you. With one voice they all cry out, 'Now you are as weak as we are!

Your might and power were buried with you. The sound of the harp in your palace has ceased. Now maggots are your sheet, and worms your blanket.'
(Isa 14:3-11, NLT).

Now, beginning at verse 12, the subject morphs into Lucifer.

"How you are fallen from heaven, O shining star, son of the morning! You have been thrown down to the earth, you who destroyed the nations of the world.

For you said to yourself, 'I will ascend to heaven and set my throne above God's stars. I will preside on the mountain of the gods far away in the north.

I will climb to the highest heavens and be like the Most High.' (Isa 14:12-14).

Beginning at verse 15, the morphing overlaps the two.

Instead, you will be brought down to the place of the dead, down to its lowest depths. ***Everyone there will stare at you and ask, 'Can this be the one who shook the earth and made the kingdoms of the world tremble?***
Is this the one who destroyed the world and made it into a wasteland? Is this the king who demolished the world's greatest cities and had no mercy on his prisoners?'

"The kings of the nations lie in stately glory, each in his own tomb, but you will be thrown out of your grave like a worthless branch. Like a corpse trampled underfoot, you will be dumped into a mass grave with those killed in battle. You will descend to the pit. You will not be given a proper burial, for you have destroyed your nation and slaughtered your people. The descendants of such an evil person will never again receive honor (Isa 14:15-20, NLT).

A fitting end to two miserable tyrants, which Revelation also confirms in various verses, including this one:

And the devil that deceived them was cast into the lake of fire and brimstone, where the beast and the false prophet are, and shall be tormented day and night for ever and ever (Rev 20:10).

What a wonderful scripture that is. And, speaking of demises, let's now look at the end of Mystery Babylon as we start wrapping up this chapter.

TEN KINGS WHO HATE THE WHORE

In writing this book, we've attempted to give a broad, but insightful, overview of the last days to equip those with ears to hear and eyes to see with enough information so that they do not get caught off guard by misguided teachings of end-time events.

And while we haven't discussed every eschatological point, we've given enough concrete facts about what to look for so that the reader could be fully armed to avoid the traps set by Antichrist. And while we haven't even fully explained what the 666 mark actually means (we do know it's not an Arabic phrase!), it doesn't matter. We've given enough clues of the Antichrist that when he does appear, you will know him even *before* the mark is issued! And, when we see 666 fully applied to Antichrist, it will only be the icing on the cake.

Now let's examine another area of mystery that will set the stage for this section of the book.

In both Revelation 13 and 17, there is a depiction of the Antichrist beast with seven heads and ten horns. We've already seen that the seven heads in Revelation 13 are a composite of the kingdoms Antichrist absorbs into his orbit and control (Dan 7). But in Revelation 17, the seven heads seem to have morphed and pivoted into other descriptive symbols at the *exact time that Jerusalem begins riding the Antichrist.*

> *And here is the mind which hath wisdom. The seven heads are seven mountains, on which the woman sitteth. And there are* (or, "they are also," NET) *seven kings: five are fallen, and one is, and the other is not yet come; and when he cometh, he must continue a short space. And the beast that was, and is not, even he is the eighth, and is of the seven, and goeth into perdition. And the ten horns which thou sawest are ten kings, which have received no kingdom as yet; but receive power as kings one hour with the beast. These have one mind, and shall give their power and strength unto the beast* (Rev 17:9-13).

"The seven heads are seven mountains on which the woman sits." Many who contend that Mystery Babylon is Rome insist that this scripture describes the *seven hills of*

Rome. But they neglect to incorporate the rest of the verse: *"And they* [the mountains or hills] *are also seven kings, five are fallen…"*

Can five of the seven hills surrounding Rome suddenly fall? Can they just disappear? Five kings can certainly fall though. But even if one insisted on a solely geographical interpretation of this verse, Jerusalem also has seven hills surrounding it as well. So this point is muted when trying to defend Rome as Mystery Babylon.

Wikipedia lists Jerusalem's seven hills in its article entitled, "List of cities claimed to be built on seven hills."

> "Jerusalem's seven hills are Mount Scopus, Mount Olivet and the Mount of Corruption (all three are peaks in a mountain ridge that lies east of the Old City), Mount Ophel, the original Mount Zion, the New Mount Zion and the hill on which the Antonia Fortress was built."

Yet the scripture maintains that the seven heads represent seven mountains, which are *kings!*

"They are also seven kings, five are fallen, and one is, and the other is not yet come." This is one of the more perplexing scriptures, and it's probably difficult to understand because it requires our living in that future time to fully digest its meaning.

There are some who contend that these kings are *not* contemporaneous, as in Daniel 7, but are a succession of kings, perhaps spanning thousands of years, i.e., five have passed, one is present, and one is to come (from the vantage point of John writing the book in the late first century).

And yet even those who support such a conclusion have no idea who the five who have fallen are. One would think that if you're going to make an argument that five of the heads of Mystery Babylon have already lived and died, and are a product of our history, then you should be able to identify the past five kings.

At this point, this may be one of those things that only comes to light in the future! To the author it seems that these kings are contemporaneous with one another, but, again, we won't know for sure until that time comes.

However, there are more compelling insights to these scriptures that we're willing to explore.

"Five are fallen, and one is, and the other is not yet come; and when he cometh, he must continue a short space." We're not speculating on who comprises the five who have fallen. The *one that is* must be the Antichrist though, as it relates this later on in the chapter:

> *And the beast that was, and is not, even he is the eighth, and is of the seven, and goeth into perdition* (Rev 17:11).

The *beast that was and is not,* as we've seen earlier, is a term denoting the resurrection "miracle" of the Antichrist. Therefore when it says that the Antichrist *is of the seven,* than he must be the *one* (head) *that is* (Rev 17:10).

And it's probable that he accounts for one head (that *is*) *before* his resurrection and another head (the eighth) *after* his resurrection.

But we are far more interested in detailing the head that *has not yet come, but when he comes must continue a short space.* Who is this head who rules for a short space? Some would say that it is the Antichrist who rules for the "short space" of the Great Tribulation. But that's three and a half years in length! There is actually another "short space" detailed in scripture, much shorter than the length of the tribulation. Specifically it's the duration of *one hour!* For scripture tells us that it's in *one hour* that Mystery Babylon is destroyed!

Let's examine the scriptures pertaining to the seventh head who destroys Jerusalem in one hour:

*And the ten horns which thou sawest are **ten kings, which have received no kingdom as yet; but receive power as kings one hour** with the beast. **These have one mind, and shall give their power and strength unto the beast** (Rev 17:12-13).*

Notice these ten horns are ten kings who have not yet received a kingdom. This seems to fulfill what it says about the last head: i.e., the ***other is not yet come.**.*

Then it says they *receive power as kings **one hour!*** Again, that fulfills the *short space* requirement imposed by the earlier scripture.

These ten kings, which we're led to believe come out of Europe, are united as having ***one mind**, and operate as one, *giving their power and strength unto the beast*, forming that seventh head. **This is the head that God will use to judge and destroy Jerusalem.**

*And the **ten horns which thou sawest upon the beast, these shall hate the whore, and shall make her desolate and naked, and shall eat her flesh, and burn her with fire.** For God hath put in their hearts to fulfil his will, and to agree, and **give their kingdom unto the beast,** until the words of God shall be fulfilled (Rev 17:16-17).*

Please note the judgment against Jerusalem lasts *one hour!*

*Standing afar off for the fear of her torment, saying, **Alas, alas, that great city Babylon, that mighty city! for in one hour is thy judgment come** (Rev 18:10)*

*And saying, Alas, alas, that great city, that was clothed in fine linen, and purple, and scarlet, and decked with gold, and precious stones, and pearls! For in **one hour** so great riches is come to nought. And every shipmaster, and all the company in ships,* *and sailors, and as many as trade by sea, stood afar off* (Rev 18:16-17)

*And they cast dust on their heads, and cried, weeping and wailing, saying, Alas, alas, **that great city, **wherein were made rich all that had ships in the sea by reason of her costliness! **for in one hour is she made desolate*** (Rev 18:19).

If we were to pinpoint the timeframe that Mystery Babylon is destroyed, it would have to be towards the end of the Day of the Lord and the end of the judgment period. The battle of Armageddon, where armies surround Jerusalem, comes just before this final death knell from the ten kings.

Revelation 14 opens up with the Lord already on Mount Zion inaugurating the 144,000 into the New Millennium, where we read:

And there followed another angel, saying, Babylon is fallen, is fallen, that great city, because she made all nations drink of the wine of the wrath of her fornication (Rev 14:8).

The timing of the Lord's arrival also coincides with the Stone striking the ten toes of Nebuchadnezzar's statue, those toes representing the last remnant of the ten kings from Europe (Roman Empire).

*And whereas thou sawest the feet and toes, part of potters' clay, and part of iron, the kingdom shall be divided ... And as the toes of the feet were part of iron, and part of clay, so the kingdom shall be partly strong, and partly broken ... **And in the days of these kings shall the God of heaven set up a kingdom, which shall never be destroyed**: and the kingdom shall not be left to other people, but it shall break in pieces and consume all these kingdoms, and it shall stand for ever* (Dan 2:41-42, 44).

As you recall, the Day of the Lord actually lasts several months, as God's wrath is unleashed against an unrepentant humanity.

And, with that, we have a good overview of Mystery Babylon. While we have tried in this volume to unveil the hidden meanings of important eschatology symbols, we know we have not covered every iota of God's Word. Regarding the two witnesses, for instance, we still have no clue as to their identity although, as Malachi suggests, one of the two witnesses would be the fulfillment of the one coming in the power and authority of Elijah!

But we did want to give the reader enough information so that they could more easily navigate the turbulent tribulation period ahead.

We feel that we've established key landmarks from which other points of eschatology can smoothly fit.

In many ways, this volume, up till now, was merely setting the stage and priming the pump for the most important chapter of the book.

10
THE GREAT ESCAPE

Prominent before Christ's return, there will be two primary characteristics of humanity: fear and faith. No matter the country, no matter the ethnicity, no matter the religion – everyone then on the earth will either quiver in fear or thrive in faith. There will be no middle ground, as everyone will be forced to decide in the prophesied *valley of decision*. The ones hit the hardest will be those who refuse to acknowledge God. As Luke shows, ***"Men's hearts* (will be) *failing them for fear,** and for looking after those things which are coming on the earth: for the powers of heaven shall be shaken* (Lk 21:26).

So fierce the struggle between light and dark forces during that time, the Lord rhetorically pondered the question, *"When I return, shall I find faith on the earth?"* (Lk 18:8).

Stop and consider the enormity and gravity of Christ's comment. We know that there will be a falling away from the faith in the last days:

> *Now the Spirit speaketh expressly, that in the latter times **some shall depart from the faith,** giving heed to seducing spirits, and doctrines of devils* (1 Tim 4:1)

*Let no man deceive you by any means: for that day shall not come, **except there come a falling away first*** (2 Thess 2:3).

This is why the word compels us to *contend* for faith.

*(I) exhort you that **ye should earnestly contend for the faith** which was once delivered unto the saints* (Jude 1:3).

Therefore it's imperative that if we're going to be living in the last days (and we've already shown there's *no* pre-tribulation rapture), we had better be growing in faith in our Lord Jesus Christ.

Later in this chapter, as we present the many varied ways the Lord protects His children from evil, we hope to increase the faith of the reader so that they will be well prepared to escape the evil brought on by Antichrist's persecution.

So then faith cometh by hearing, and hearing by the word of God (Rom 10:17).

Let us first encourage the reader by presenting an overview of the condition of the Church in the last days, and the promises of protection for one of the churches.

THE LAST DAYS CHURCH

Many erroneously contend that the reason why the Church is no longer mentioned after Revelation 4 is because the Church is already raptured. But that's not the case at all. They are not mentioned because – *suddenly* – once the Great Tribulation arrives on the scene, they have to flee persecution and go *underground*. This is why they are suddenly referred to as *saints* throughout the rest of the book, and no longer as the Church. They've been scattered.

Revelation 2 and 3 give an overview of the seven churches that were originally founded in the early days of Acts. Each church was birthed along a somewhat circular Roman mail route in the area we know today as Turkey.

Not only were they actual churches at that time, with unique strengths and weaknesses, but they also served as prototypes for churches that would surface throughout time until the return of Christ.

We contend that at least four of the seven churches are definitely on the earth at the time when Jesus returns. This will positively dispel the notion that the church is no longer mentioned after Revelation 4. Let's look at the last four churches: Thyatira, Sardis, Philadelphia, Laodicea.

> *And unto the angel of the **church in Thyatira** write; These things saith the Son of God, who hath his eyes like unto a flame of fire, and his feet are like fine brass; I know thy works, and charity, and service, and faith, and thy patience, and thy works; and the last to be more than the first. Notwithstanding I have a few things against thee, because thou sufferest that woman Jezebel, which calleth herself a prophetess, to teach and to seduce my servants to commit fornication, and to eat things sacrificed unto idols. And I gave her space to repent of her fornication; and she repented not. **Behold, I will cast her into a bed, and them that commit adultery with her into Great Tribulation, except they repent of their deeds.** And I will kill her children with death; and all the churches shall know that I am he which searcheth the reins and hearts: and I will give unto every one of you according to your works* (Rev 2:18-23).

Notice what Jesus is saying to Thyatira. If they do not repent of allowing that Jezebel spirit to operate within the church, He will cause them to go into the Great Tribulation. This is the same *Great Tribulation* that Jesus refers to when

He says, *For then shall be **great tribulation**, such as was not since the beginning of the world to this time, no, nor ever shall be.* (Mt 24:21).

In both instances, it is the same Greek phrase: *megas thlipsis.* **There cannot be two Great Tribulations that are worse than any other!** Jesus is saying that if they don't repent, they will be going into the Great Tribulation.

I pray that people's eyes are opened to the clear word in scripture!

> *And unto the angel of the **church in Sardis** write; These things saith he that hath the seven Spirits of God, and the seven stars; I know thy works, that thou hast a name that thou livest, and art dead. Be watchful, and strengthen the things which remain, that are ready to die: for I have not found thy works perfect before God. Remember therefore how thou hast received and heard, and hold fast, and repent. **If therefore thou shalt not watch, I will come on thee as a thief, and thou shalt not know what hour I will come upon thee*** (Rev 3:1-3).

We've already discussed *the thief in the night* metaphor and how that watchful Christians need not be caught unaware by the return of Christ. But some slothful Christians will most definitely wake up to shocking reality when the *thief in the night* comes upon them when they're not prepared.

This metaphor, given to the Sardis church, makes no sense, *unless* the Sardis church is on the earth at the time Christ returns. In other words, Christ cannot come as *a thief in the night* to a church that isn't around when He returns.

Now that we've established that Sardis is on the earth in the last days, let's see what Christ says about the next two churches.

> *And to the angel of the **church in Philadelphia** write; These things saith he that is holy, he that is true, he*

*that hath the key of David, he that openeth, and no man shutteth; and shutteth, and no man openeth; I know thy works: behold, I have set before thee an open door, and no man can shut it: for thou hast a little strength, and hast kept my word, and hast not denied my name ... **Because thou hast kept the word of my patience, I also will keep thee from the hour of temptation** [i.e., trial or testing], **which shall come upon all the world, to try them that dwell upon the earth. Behold, I come quickly: hold that fast which thou hast, that no man take thy crown** (Rev 3:7-11).*

The Philadelphia church is the most highly regarded of all seven churches, even more highly regarded than the first-named church, Ephesus, which actually can distinguish itself from the others by being the only church to have an epistle addressed to it.

Hold onto this next thought for later – but is it possible that the Philadelphia church is more highly regarded than Ephesus because of the one component that Jesus says is greater than all? *Love?*

Philadelphia actually comes from the Greek word meaning *brotherly love.* Meanwhile Ephesus was berated for having *lost their first love* (Rev 2:4).

And, being so highly regarded, Christ makes this promise to them: *Because thou hast kept the word of my patience, I also will keep thee from the hour of temptation, which shall come upon all the world, to try them that dwell upon the earth.*

By now, no one can misread this verse. *The hour of temptation that will come upon all the world* is nothing short of the Great Tribulation.

Here God promises to protect the Philadelphia church from the Great Tribulation. But remember *protecting them from* does not mean *taking them out of,* as in a rapture. Christ makes that very same distinction when He prayed about the Church to the Father on the last night before He gave His life:

I pray not that thou shouldest take them out of the world, but that thou shouldest keep them from the evil (one) (Jn 17:15).

Either God means what He says, or He doesn't. God promises to protect this particular church as the world is going through major testing. We're going to find that the Bible offers hope for this day and hour, as we examine scripture after scripture which details extraordinary examples of God's supernatural ability to sustain, protect, empower the remnant of His people that He holds dear. And those scriptures are for us today, that we may have hope in God's protection.

*For whatsoever things were written aforetime were written for our learning, that we through **patience** and comfort of the scriptures might have hope* (Rom 15:4).

We will soon go into those scriptures, but let us proceed step by step. Please note that word *patience* in the above verse. We find that God uses that same word when addressing the Philadelphia church: *Because you have kept the word of My patience.* What does that imply? In both cases, the word *patience* comes from the same Greek word meaning *endurance, steadfastness, perseverance,* or *steadfast waiting for.* Specifically, there is an even exchange between the Philadelphia church and God, i.e., because the Philadelphia church keeps the word of His patience (they've endured, they're steadfast, they're persevering, they're not giving up, they're hoping beyond hope in God's redemption), God will protect them during the worst time of trouble on the earth. This promise is ironclad and immutable. It brings to mind another scripture:

*But he that shall **endure** unto the end, the same shall*

*be **saved*** (Mt 24:13).

Interestingly enough, the word for *endure* comes from the very same Greek word just used for *patience*. The context is the same as before. These people are patiently enduring, steadfastly persevering, hoping beyond hope in God's protection and deliverance during tough times.

Romans, incidentally, also uses the same word for *patience* in the phrase *patient in tribulation* (Rom 12:12), denoting the firm connection between patience and tribulation.

Notice also the word *saved* in the above verse. It comes from the Greek word *sozo,* which is a wonderful, all-around, purposeful word with meanings ranging from salvation to healing to deliverance to protection. The core root of this word, however, actually means to be *safe!* Strong's Concordance offers this as sozo's primary definition, *to save, keep safe and sound, to rescue from danger or destruction.*

Christ admonishes these to patiently endure, like the Philadelphians, until *the end!* The end is, of course, the end of this age, when Jesus finally returns. Therefore, if these Christians are enduring until Christ's return, they are *enduring* throughout the Great Tribulation! And, thus, God has spared and protected them from Antichrist's wrath.

However, as we've said before, some will give glory to God by enduring and being preserved throughout the Great Tribulation, but others will give glory to God by laying down their lives.

Even Christ Himself, in the Olivet Prophecy, describes in effect two groups of Christians in the end times. Some will be martyred (*they shall kill you*, Mt 24:9) and some will be protected (*those who endure to the end will be saved*, Mt 24:13), the latter being those in the Philadelphia church.

Let's take a look now at the Laodicea church, and see how it compares to the Philadelphia church.

*And unto the angel of the **church of the Laodiceans** write; These things saith the Amen, the faithful and true witness, the beginning of the creation of God; I know thy works, that thou art neither cold nor hot: I would thou wert cold or hot. So then because thou art lukewarm, and neither cold nor hot, I will spue thee out of my mouth. Because thou sayest, I am rich, and increased with goods, and have need of nothing; and knowest not that thou art wretched, and miserable, and poor, and blind, and naked: **I counsel thee to buy of me gold tried in the fire, that thou mayest be rich; and white raiment, that thou mayest be clothed, and that the shame of thy nakedness do not appear; and anoint thine eyes with eyesalve, that thou mayest see.** As many as I love, I rebuke and chasten: be zealous therefore, and repent* (Rev 3:14-19).

This church is found to be lacking in so many basic Christian attributes, Christ is about to vomit her out of His mouth. Her refusal to be on fire for the Lord compels God to force them into the fire of tribulation. Her lackadaisical attitude in loving God forces Him to throw her into the valley of decision, where she must choose between Christ and Antichrist – even if it leads to martyrdom. God will mercifully allow them any circumstance if it leads to their salvation.

His ultimate aim is expressed in 1 Peter:

That the trial of your faith, being much more precious than of gold that perisheth, though it be tried with fire, might be found unto praise and honour and glory at the appearing of Jesus Christ (1 Pet 1:7).

And yet God will be with them, perfecting their character, throughout this time. And the Holy Spirit will guide them when they are brought to courts to put their faith on trial.

> *But before all these, they shall lay their hands on you, and persecute you, delivering you up to the synagogues, and into prisons, being brought before kings and rulers for my name's sake. And it shall turn to you for a testimony. Settle it therefore in your hearts, not to meditate before what ye shall answer: For I will give you a mouth and wisdom, which all your adversaries shall not be able to gainsay nor resist* (Lk 21:12-15).

Some of these Christians, who have had no visible achievements in their Christian walk, will have arrived at the pinnacle of their life's work by simply standing up for Jesus amid great opposition from the Antichrist.

"Well done," says the Lord, "My good and faithful servants," as they are received into eternal glory.

Now let's review. We've just seen how that the last four churches of Revelation are all on the earth at the time of Antichrist. Thyatira was warned about suffering in the Great Tribulation. Sardis was warned that Christ could come as a *thief in the night* in their lifetime. Philadelphia was given a promise that they would be protected from the Great Tribulation. And Laodicea was given a demand for perfection in fiery tribulation.

WHAT TO MAKE OF THIS?

What can we learn from Christ's admonitions to the Philadelphia and Laodicea churches? What can we learn from the characteristics exhibited by the two churches? Why is one given protection status and the other not?

Let's compare scripture to scripture and see if we can arrive at an accurate assessment.

We know for certain that Jesus promises to protect the Philadelphia church. We know that it is probably the most highly favored church of all. What are some of its characteristics? The Philadelphia church had two major characteristics that set it apart from the others.

Its very name, Philadelphia, means *brotherly love*. More than anything else, the Lord values love as being the motivating factor in all we do. Everything hinges on love. Works alone are valueless without the foundation of love at its core.

> *If I could speak all the languages of earth and of angels, but didn't love others, I would only be a noisy gong or a clanging cymbal. If I had the gift of prophecy, and if I understood all of God's secret plans and possessed all knowledge, and if I had such faith that I could move mountains, but didn't love others, I would be nothing. If I gave everything I have to the poor and even sacrificed my body, I could boast about it; but if I didn't love others, I would have gained nothing* (1 Cor 13:1-3, NLT).

Such was the mighty testimony of the Philadelphia church, which is highly valued by Jesus Christ.

An interesting side note is that the Apostle John, the one whom Jesus loved and the Apostle known for his love, was the only Apostle not to have been martyred. All the others were.

In fact, legend has it that the Apostle John was dropped in a vat of boiling oil before a blood-lusted crowd in Rome's Coliseum, or possibly nearby at the Latin Gate, for refusing to denounce his faith. Not only didn't he denounce his faith, but he continued preaching as he was lowered into the boiling oil. When he miraculously came out unscathed, many became converted to the true God.

From there he was banished to the Isle of Patmos, from where he received a measure of safety, and from where he wrote the book of Revelation.

The *Key of David* is the second distinguishing factor for

the Philadelphia church. But what is the Key of David? Let's review what Christ said to the Philadelphia church.

> *These things saith he that is holy, he that is true, **he that hath the key of David, he that openeth, and no man shutteth; and shutteth, and no man openeth;** I know thy works: behold, **I have set before thee an open door, and no man can shut it:** for thou hast a little strength, and hast kept my word, and hast not denied my name* (Rev 3:7-8).

We know from this verse that the Lord Jesus holds the Key of David and gives it to whomever He chooses, and then *they* have the authority to open and close. In this case, He gives authority to the Philadelphia church, in the same way that He gave Peter the Keys to the Kingdom.

The first time in which scripture uses the term *Key of David* is in Isaiah 22. That chapter refers to the impending judgment against Jerusalem and the removal of the wicked and proud Shebna, the treasonous treasurer and chief officer in the court of King Hezekiah of Judah. Shebna cruelly enriched himself at the expense of Judah, and God was not pleased. The Lord was going to replace Shebna with Eliakim and it was to Eliakim that God gave the Key of David.

> *And it shall come to pass in that day, that I will call my servant Eliakim the son of Hilkiah: And I will clothe him with thy robe, and strengthen him with thy girdle, and I will commit thy government into his hand: and he shall be a father to the inhabitants of Jerusalem, and to the house of Judah. **And the key of the house of David will I lay upon his shoulder; so he shall open, and none shall shut; and he shall shut, and none shall open*** (Isa 22:20-22).

This is the changing of the guard. God is replacing Shebna with Eliakim and stripping Shebna from his authority and placing it on Eliakim. Once again, this key denotes authority, kingly authority! At the behest of kings, decrees are issued and put forth into motion that none can withstand. Doors are opened which none can close, and closed which none can open.

Therefore the Philadelphia church has heaven-sent keys and extraordinary power to knock down spiritual doors with spiritual battering rams, to break through spiritual resistance in the heavenlies and to advance the Kingdom of God on the earth.

Those two qualities are supreme in describing the Philadelphia church.

Meanwhile, how does the Laodicea church differ? Unfortunately, it seems like it couldn't care less about love to God and to fellow man nor about doing anything supernatural for the Lord. It's lazy, poor, blind, naked. It doesn't even care to carry the mantle of the Key of David and do extraordinary works of service. It actually sounds like typical Americans who have no real regard for God – maybe they have an outward show for God, but nothing really from the heart.

Consider this: one church is protected in the Great Tribulation, the other is not. One church is zealous for God and His work, the other is not.

Does that say anything about how you should live your life? Let this be a call to righteousness to everyone reading this now. It is time now to draw more closely to Jesus Christ than ever before. Seek His face while He is near. Call upon His name and make a demand upon yourself that you will submit to Him and His ways. Ask, plead, petition for His guidance. Get close enough to Him so that you can hear His voice and be guided by Him. The only way to fully prepare yourself from the impending crises in the world is to follow His voice.

No amount of armaments, foodstuff or water stored will prepare and sustain us for what is to come. Suppose if the area one is holding all his provision is attacked and destroyed? Suppose the Lord wants you to move to another area for his purposes? The only *sure escape* is the protection of God, through hearing His voice and following His directions.

ANTICHRIST IN PHILADELPHIA WORD

The most mysterious verse in Jesus' charge to the Philadelphia church is this:

> *Behold, I will make them of the synagogue of Satan, which say they are Jews, and are not, but do lie; behold, I will make them to come and worship before thy feet, and to know that I have loved thee* (Rev 3:9).

What in the world is the *synagogue of Satan?* Obviously, it is a false, religious institution that leads to death and hell, led by Satan. It is a counterfeit religion, with a counterfeit messiah. *They say they are Jews and are not.* Salvation is of the Jews, and they are bringing none into salvation.

This synagogue of Satan can be none other than Antichrist's reign on the earth, which is leading the world to hell at the same time that Philadelphia church is thriving.

Let's go back to Isaiah. We've already seen the connection between the Philadelphia church and Eliakim (i.e., they both have the key of David). Now let's see the connection between Shebna and the Antichrist. In both passages, God rejects the Antichrist symbols to make way for the Lord's preferred replacement (i.e., Eliakim and the Philadelphia church).

Notice in this passage how Shebna becomes a type of Antichrist. The Lord denounces that self-seeking official Shebna, whose reign over Jerusalem was oppressive:

> *Thus says the Lord GOD of hosts, "Come, go to this steward, to Shebna, who is over the household, and*

say to him: What have you to do here and whom have you here, that you have hewn here a tomb for yourself, you who hew a tomb on the height, and carve a habitation for yourself in the rock? **Behold, the LORD will hurl you away violently, O you strong man. He will seize firm hold on you, and whirl you round and round, and throw you like a ball into a wide land; there you shall die, and there shall be your splendid chariots, you shame of your master's house. I will thrust you from your office, and you will be cast down from your station** (Isa 22:15-19, RSV).

Sounds very much like how God is going to violently remove the Antichrist and thrust him into the bottomless pit. The reference to Shebna building a tomb for himself is a metaphor. He didn't actually build a tomb but, in God's viewpoint, all of his selfish ambition and quest for power to lord it over Jerusalem was as good as building a tomb for himself.

Just like the Antichrist.

Let's recap. God, indeed, promises Philadelphia church such extraordinary protection throughout Antichrist's rule and He also offers them a substantial authority on the earth – despite Satan's control of the world as the god of this world (2 Cor 4:4). Yet this church is given a kingly authority to open and close doors and to break through the walls imposed by the Satanic realm.

READER, BE PREPARED!

All of which brings us to the most encouraging part of this book. Everything written in this volume, up till this page, was to prepare the reader for this truth.

Get ready to enlarge your imagination, increase your faith, and boost your expectations. This is the new paradigm for the Church today. For decades, we've been believing what some ministers have told us, that we wouldn't be on earth at the time Antichrist rises to power. But we've been believing a lie. We've seen in the scriptures that this isn't true. So rather than holding onto the false hope of the pre-trib rapture, let us hold fast to the sure word of God.

God has given us many promises in His word for divine protection. In the worst of times, God is present to protect us, guide us, offer routes of escape, provide needed sustenance, move miraculously on our behalf, dispatch legions of angels for any situation.

The scriptures offer tons of examples of God intervening in the lives of His people. Everything written in scripture has been written for us, down to our day and age, as a clear indication of how God will act on *our* behalf too.

1 Corinthians says:

> *These things happened to them as examples and were written for our instruction, on whom the ends of the ages have come ... No trial has overtaken you that is not faced by others. And God is faithful: He will not let you be tried beyond what you are able to bear, but with the trial will also provide a way out so that you may be able to endure it* (1 Cor 10:11, 13, NET).

And no matter where we are on the earth at the time Antichrist rises to power, God can offer each person their own bubble of protection, their own place of safety, so that no harm comes to them.

Let us not think that those who survive the Great Tribulation did so through happenstance. It's far better to be in God's will than it is to hope for happenstance.

Remember, God commends the Philadelphia church, which is based on *brotherly love*. Yes, Hope is important because it's the bedrock of Faith. And Faith is important because without it we cannot please the Lord. But the greatest of these three is Love (1 Cor 13:13).

If you are determined to love God and His ways far more than you love yourself and your ways, and you accept Jesus as your Lord and Guide, then you'll receive the Lord's attention and everything He will do for you will be for your good – even during the tough times ahead.

Yet, no matter how much you love God, you will be in awe if you came to understand and live by the immeasurable love God has for you. May the veil be taken off our eyes so that we can see the enormity of His love and concern for each one of us as His children. May we come to understand that His love for us is greater than any physical trouble ahead.

Before continuing this chapter, try to fix into your heart the fact that **everything God does is because of His love for us – yes, for *you*, in particular.** Your love for Him, your love for others is only a meager reflection of God's supernatural love for *you!*

In order to get through the tough times ahead, you're going to have to absorb into your heart the fact that God loves you and that He will make a way out for you. And even if He doesn't, His love for you will sustain you no matter what happens. Our physical lives are only temporary but our faith in Christ will translate us into eternal sons and daughters of God from where we will never again be subjected to the wrath of Satan.

FROM GOD'S ARSENAL OF MIRACLES

The Word of God is replete with miracle after miracle showing how God protects, sustains, and nourishes His people – usually at times when they have no other way out. Those examples are for our encouragement for the days ahead. If God did it for them, He can do it for us. Let this chapter serve to build our faith, because it is going to be our faith that will empower God to fulfill these things we believe

Him for.

Since there are so many examples to choose from, we've decided to list the Top Ten exemplary passages from the scriptures that should bolster one's faith in God's supernatural love for His people, even during tough times.

1 – Jesus Just *Disappears*

It seems that nothing enrages a religious crowd more than the Word of God. Jesus was just beginning His ministry when He returned to a synagogue in His hometown of Nazareth. He opened the book of Isaiah and began reading a prophecy that was the fulfillment of His very ministry (and if truth be known, the ministry of every true believer!).

It spoke about how He had come to release the captives, preach the gospel, heal the sick, etc. The authority by which the Lord spoke these words made His fellow countrymen condescendingly ask, "Isn't this Joseph's son?" Their inability to accept this local boy as a Prophet caused Jesus to indict them: "No prophet is accepted in his own town!"

After He uses scriptural examples showing how local people have always missed out on what God is doing, the religious people were filled with wrath!

They violently took hold of Jesus, forced Him to the precipice of the city in order to hurl him headlong into His death. Then the scriptures understate the miraculous nature of the next line: *But he passing through the midst of them went his way* (Luke 4:30).

What?! What do you mean *passing through the midst of them?* Did He disappear? Did God blind their eyes so that they couldn't see Him? Did God confuse their minds? Was He translated?

Who knows?

But God protected Jesus through miraculous means, and He can protect us likewise. Think on this the next time you're surrounded by enemies with no place to go. [Related scriptures: Lk 4:16–30; Jn 8:20, 59; 10:39].

2 – We're "Asbestos" Can Be

No scriptural reference more profoundly parallels the remarkable way that God will protect saints in the Philadelphia church from Antichrist than this one – the story of Shadrach, Meshach and Abednego.

All of the Antichrist symbols are strongly evident in this Old Testament prototype. We have an Antichrist figure, Nebuchadnezzar, the King of *Babylon*, demanding worship from each individual in the world he controls. People are commanded to worship this Antichrist *image* (of the beast), set up to represent the King, or face death! We have people betraying God's people to death (Mt 24:10). And we have God's people looking to God for divine deliverance.

Oh – if we only had the faith of Shadrach, Meshach and Abednego for the days ahead of us now!

Upon hearing of their refusal to worship the image, the King angrily summoned them to him. The King, sneeringly and contemptuously, looked down on them, demanding to know whether Shadrach, Meshach and Abednego would humble themselves to worship the image once the music commenced.

> *O Nebuchadnezzar, we do not need to defend ourselves before you. If we are thrown into the blazing furnace, the God whom we serve is able to save us. He will rescue us from your power, Your Majesty. But even if he doesn't, we want to make it clear to you, Your Majesty, that we will never serve your gods or worship the gold statue you have set up* (Dan 3:16-18, NLT).

The King was furious and commanded the fiery furnace to be heated seven times hotter than usual. Guards threw the three bound servants of God into the fiery furnace. So hot was the furnace that it killed the guards instantly.

And looking through the smoke-filled, bright-hot

furnace, the King could make out what appeared to be Shadrach, Meshach and Abednego walking about freely, unbound, in the flames of fire – and they were totally unhurt!

And there also appeared someone *else* in the fire – someone the King described as like the *Son of God!*

Miraculously, the preincarnate Jesus appeared, causing not a hair on their heads to be singed, nor their clothes to be burned nor reeking of smoke.

Such is the power of the Living God to protect His children through any circumstance, even under the most impossible duress and Satanic oppression.

This was not just God protecting them *from*, but God protecting them *in* – in the same way that God protected John the Apostle while *in* the boiling vat of oil.

Yet after their ordeal, Shadrach, Meshach and Abednego were promoted to high office, in the same way that the end-time saints will, after their ordeal, become kings and priests and rule over the earth (Rev 1:6; 5:10; Mt 19:28).

This is, indeed, the most compelling prototype of how God can protect His people during the Antichrist reign. May we have the faith of Shadrach, Meshach and Abednego where we can state defiantly, "God is able to deliver us from this death sentence, but even if He doesn't, we will not bow down to this image." [Related scriptures: Dan 3:1-30; Isa 43:2].

3 – Daniel the Lion Tamer

Satan uses the same ol' tired tricks from time immemorial. Nothing seems to change but the characters and the location. And, in the same way that Satan tried to kill off Shadrach, Meshach and Abednego during the Babylonian period, Satan tried to kill off Daniel in the Medo-Persian period – and by using the same methods.

Daniel was one of three top leaders directly under King Darius, but Daniel's unusual anointing made him stand out above the other two. He was definitely walking the walk, so that there was nothing incriminating to be found in him despite the many attempts by Satan's minions in the government to find something – *anything!*

So they had to make something up. And doesn't that sound just like today's political parties and modern news media?! Like we said, Satan uses the same ol' tired tricks over and over again.

Knowing full well that Daniel prayed three times a day, those minions then decided to criminalize something good and decent – prayer!

They cunningly spoke to the King and urged him to enact the death penalty for the next thirty days to anyone praying to any God "except to *you* O King" (heavy sarcasm, no doubt, dripped from these treacherous brown-nosers).

The incredible thing about Daniel was that once he heard of the decree, it didn't faze him in the least. He bravely continued to pray to His God three times a day with his windows opened toward Jerusalem and, even at the threat of death for praying, his prayers were filled with *thankfulness!*

There will be a slight pause in the narrative so as to digest that last statement.

True to form, once the law was enacted, a mob assembled to catch Daniel in the heinous act of praying. When they did, they coerced the King to apply the law immediately.

King Darius wasn't exactly supportive of losing his top administrator to hungry lions, but reluctantly he signed off on the execution with this hopeful salutation, "The God that you serve, He will save you!"

And Daniel was thrown into the lion's den.

Ashamed and remorseful became the King, to the point that he could not sleep at all. Hurriedly, he approached the lion's den, calling out, "Daniel, did your God save you?"

Imagine his relief when he heard Daniel's cheery reply, "O King, live for ever!"

My God sent his angel and closed the lions' mouths
so that they have not harmed me, because I was
found to be innocent before him. Nor have I done
any harm to you, O king" (Dan 6:22, NET).

So, once again, scripture shows that God can protect His
people under the most strenuous circumstances. Faith comes
by hearing, and hearing by the Word of God.

It is important that with the rise of Antichrist, God's
people may continue to hold fast their firm relationship with
God and offer the same passionate praise that Daniel did in
the worst of circumstances. For many of God's people will,
indeed, be shielded in bubbles of protection so that they may
be alive when Jesus returns. [Related scriptures: Dan 6:1-
28].

4 – On the Wings of Eagles

If there was ever an example where God performed miracle
after miracle in order to convince a people of His love and
protection during great adversity and overwhelming odds, it is
the story of the Exodus.

And if there was ever an Old Testament prototype that
exactly parallels the Christians' miraculous entrance into the
promised land of Christ's Millennium, it is this one as well.
Notice the many parallels:

- Pharaoh is a type of Antichrist
- Pharaoh/Antichrist want to control/bring to subjection God's people
- God gives around-the-clock protection upon His people through many supernatural signs, wonders and miracles
- God even uses the earth and sea to miraculously protect His people
- As soon as God's people are removed from danger,

judgments come down on their enemies;
* God leads His people into their rightful inheritance

Additionally, Revelation 12 speaks of two groups of Christians under persecution by the enemy. The first group is given *eagles wings* in order to escape the grasp of the Antichrist forces. The other is not (Rev 12:13-17).

Interestingly enough, that phrase *eagles wings* occurs in one other passage of scripture. And, in fact, it's a metaphor that God uses to explain how He protected his people during the Exodus!

> *And Moses went up unto God, and the LORD called unto him out of the mountain, saying, Thus shalt thou say to the house of Jacob, and tell the children of Israel;* **Ye have seen what I did unto the Egyptians, and how I bare you on eagles' wings, and brought you unto myself.** *Now therefore, if ye will obey my voice indeed, and keep my covenant, then ye shall be a peculiar treasure unto me above all people: for all the earth is mine:* **And ye shall be unto me a kingdom of priests, and an holy nation.** *These are the words which thou shalt speak unto the children of Israel* (Ex 19:3-6).

Such a powerful parallel for our day! So that phrase *eagles wings* is a metaphor for all the miraculous acts associated with the Exodus, which He promises to do for Christians today!

To top it all off, after all is said and done, God even gives them the promise of becoming a *kingdom of priests* as He gives to Christians during the Millennial reign (Rev 1:6; 5:10).

But in both instances (the Exodus and Antichrist's reign), God's *eagles wings* protect His people and destroy His enemies, even through the extraordinary means of causing the earth and the sea to perform His will (Ex 15:4; Rev 12:16). [Related scriptures: Rev 12:13-17; Ex 19:4; Isa 40:28-31].

5 – There are more for us than against us

The entire military might of the Syrian army was rendered helpless by just one lone prophet of God, Elisha. Syria was in a state of war with Israel and every time they would plan an ambush against them, Israel's army was alerted and avoided the attack.

The King of Syria demanded to know who was the traitorous leaker amid their group. His aides affirmed their innocence, laying the blame on the prophet Elisha: "Why, he even knows the things you say in secret in your bedroom!"

Thus the king's wrath was kindled and he sent his army to the town of Dothan to find Elisha and kill him.

The next morning troops, horses and chariots literally surrounded Dothan.

Elisha's servant awoke to this fearsome presence. Rattled, worried and frightened, the servant cried out to Elisha, "What shall we do?"

Poised, calm and matter-of-factly, Elisha prayed to God, "Lord, open up his eyes that he may see."

Suddenly, the servant was able to see into the spiritual realm and saw up along the hillside. It was filled with an angelic army of warhorses and fiery chariots.

Suffice it to say, Elisha and his servant were protected from this vast army.

Two things to take away from this story.

1) It is imperative that we learn to hear the voice of God, for the Holy Spirit was sent to lead, guide, comfort and direct us. He warns us of things to come (Jn 16:13), so that we can avoid destruction.

2) Consider and meditate on the vast invisible army of angels that are sent for our protection.

For he shall give his angels charge over thee, to keep thee in all thy ways. They shall bear thee up in their hands, lest thou dash thy foot against a stone (Ps

91:11-12)

The angel of the LORD encampeth round about them that fear him, and delivereth (rescues) *them (Ps 34:7).*

May we have eyes to see and hearts to believe in God's powerful array of angelic resources at our disposal. God promises that there are *ministering spirits sent forth to minister for them who shall be heirs of salvation* (Heb 1:14). [Related scriptures: 2 Kings 6:8-23].

6 – Supernatural Transport
As humans, we tend to believe that there is an impenetrable wall of limitations placed on us due to time, matter and space. We forget that God created time, matter and space and can usurp their limitations at will.

Did you know that something as modern and Sci-Fi as supernatural transport was actually done by God's servants in scripture? It wasn't done often, but it's an incredible example of how God can bend the physical laws of time, matter and space and whisk someone off instantly to a distant location.

Supernatural transport is depicted in both the Old and New Testaments. As usual, the Bible tends to downplay these incidents, as if they were just run-of-the-mill miracles in the extraordinary world of Christian ministry.

Philip the Evangelist was going about his daily ministry outreach by listening to the Holy Spirit and following His directions. He was led to an Ethiopian eunuch and baptized him. Then, the scripture simply says:

And when they were come up out of the water, the Spirit of the Lord caught away Philip, that the eunuch saw him no more: and he went on his way rejoicing. But Philip was found at Azotus: and passing through he preached in all the cities, till he came to Caesarea (Acts 8:39-40).

Miraculously, the Spirit of the Lord caught up Philip and transported him to his next ministry encounter. This was not unlike the frequent-flier miles Elijah accumulated during his sojourns on earth.

There are no limitations in time, matter or space to the supernatural. Of course this was all done at the Lord's discretion and it is not something we can conjure up ourselves. But, all in all, it is definitely interesting to let our imaginations entertain the exciting possibilities in the realm of the Spirit. [Related scriptures: 1 Kings 18:12; 2 Kings 2:1-11; Acts 8:38-40].

7 – Faster Than a Speeding Chariot

God loves contests between good and evil, because He always wins. When the Antichrist teams up with the False Prophet to deceive the world during the Great Tribulation with their counterfeit signs and wonders, He will also have a duo called the Two Witnesses who will serve as a Godly counterpoint – so that people will have no excuse for their acceptance of the mark of the beast!

These titanic struggles between the sorcerers of Satan and the Prophets of God have already occurred several times in history, specifically the time when Moses confronted the Egyptian magicians during the Exodus and when the Prophet Elijah confronted the prophets of Baal on Mount Carmel.

Interestingly enough, the scriptures point to a future confrontation between good and evil when it says that someone in the spirit and power of Elijah will be sent before the Day of the Lord.

Nevertheless, there was an incident which we shall now draw upon which again shows how God can intentionally defy the natural laws He created in order to benefit His servants.

Earlier we referenced supernatural transportation, where the Lord would whisk someone off in a whirlwind to get them from Point A to Point B *fast*. Well, God has lots of miracles in His arsenal. When needed, He can give His servants the ability to outrun Secretariat in the Kentucky Derby. He did it for Elijah.

Israel had become apostate in rejecting the God of Abraham, Isaac and Jacob, and instead had begun to sacrifice their children in rituals to Baal.

Since the people assumed that Baal controlled the seasons and the weather, God, through His prophet, proclaimed that there would be no rain upon the land until they repented.

[This ability to control the weather will also be a key miracle in the ministry of the Two Witnesses.]

Then came the mighty confrontation between Elijah and the prophets of Baal. They would each place a sacrificial animal upon an altar. The sacrifice on which the Lord responded by fire would reveal the real prophets.

All day long the Baal prophets pleaded and cajoled their god to answer by fire, and he did not.

Then Elijah and his prophets set up their sacrifice and doused the altar several times with water to further humiliate Baal.

Then with a simple appeal to heaven that God would reveal Himself, "Whoosh!" came the fire of God upon the altar! This proved to all that God is God, and there is none like Him. Thus, the prophets of Baal were promptly rounded up and annihilated.

Now Elijah could pray for the rain to replenish the land. He had his servant Ahab to check seven times for signs of rain clouds in the sky.

When a small, tiny black cloud began forming a distance away, Elijah told Ahab, "You better prepare your chariot and get out of here. This rain will be so fierce you don't want to get caught in it."

As Ahab dashed out in his chariot for the city of Jezreel, the scriptures matter-of-factly state, *And the hand of the*

*LORD was on Elijah; and he girded up his loins, **and ran
before Ahab to the entrance of Jezreel*** (1 Kings 18:46)!

Elijah outran the horse and chariot! It is incredible to
consider that God is indeed all-powerful and all-loving. He
controls the weather and the forces of nature, and He prepares
good things for those who love him.

1 Kings 18:21 is a prototype for what the Two Witnesses
will tell the Antichrist followers: *How long halt ye between
two opinions? if the LORD be God, follow him: but if Baal,
then follow him.*   [Related scriptures: Ex 7, 8, 9; 1 Kings
17:1; 18:20-46; Mal 4:5-6; Mt 17:10-13; Rev 11:3-13].

8 – "Walk on....Walk on...*Water!?*"

We tend to forget that Jesus desires that everything He did in
His earthly ministry should be replicated by His people now.

Every miracle, every deliverance, every act (including
raising the dead) should be a normal function of the
Christian experience.

One of the most incredible feats of His ministry, and
there were many, was His casual stroll on water.

While other miracles seem to occur from persuasive
necessity, this one was so carefree, so bereft of urgency, that
God seems to be tickling our imaginations to believe Him
for more from His unlimited arsenal of miracles.

For, if you remember, it wasn't only Jesus who walked
on water but Peter did also!

The disciples had been instructed by Christ to go by
boat to Bethsaida. Christ, meanwhile, went up to a solitary
place to pray.

When evening had come, the winds upon the Sea of
Galilee had caused the rowing to become more difficult. But
then, piercing through the darkness, came a troubling image.

"What in the world is *that* walking toward us?" the
disciples wondered.

Being experienced fishermen, they became more
frightened by this vision than by the turbulent weather.

Then, suddenly, through the dissipating mist, the smiling face of the Savior becomes apparent. And, the countenance of the disciples quickly changes from horror to wonderment.

Peter was so fascinated by this miracle that he urged the Savior to allow him to experience this marvel as well.

"Come," was the instant reply.

Amid the tossing of the waves and the beating of the wind, Peter takes his first step on the impenetrable surface of the water.

The sea's composition had not changed at all. What had changed was that the forces of nature now had to obey the Creator of the universe. Wherever Peter now walked on the sea – so long as his focus was on the Lord – the water surface had to oblige and hold him up. It was this kind of faith that sustained him. The phrase made famous by Apollo astronaut Neil Armstrong is more aptly applied here: "One small step for man, one giant leap for mankind."

That *giant leap for mankind* is the knowledge that faith in Jesus can allow us to do the impossible. It was only when Peter turned his eyes away from Jesus and he began focusing on the mind-altering circumstances around him that his faith turned to fear and he began to sink.

More than anything, from here on end, Jesus wants us to believe Him for the impossible. [Related scriptures: Mk 6:45-53; Mt 14:22-34; Jn 6:15-21].

9 – 3 ½ Years of Freeze-Dried Vegetable Rotini?

Some who see the writing on the wall about the last days have systematically been stockpiling foodstuff and preparing their end-time bunker to wade out the Great Tribulation.

The problem, however, is that it's awfully difficult to adequately stockpile 3 ½ years of food, 3 ½ years of water, 3 ½ years of ammunition, 3 ½ years of toilet tissue, 3 ½ years of fuel for power generator, etc.

And, even if you did stockpile all of this Armageddon

equipment into your bunker, suppose radiation hit your area and you had to evacuate to a safer region?

While no one is dismissing a wise man's preparation for minor periods of shortages ahead, we'd just like to point out the impracticality of sustaining one's life for an extended period of time.

Thankfully, there are promises in the scriptures that show God's faithfulness in providing sustenance for His people. We're either going to be comforted by the hope contained in the scriptures or we're going to brood in fear as we bury our dehydrated Beef Stroganoff with Noodles in the front yard.

Thankfully, God is Master at bending the rules of the natural physical universe and providing sustenance for His people. Jesus knows this so well that when He sent out His disciples, He told them not to take anything with them – they had to learn to *trust God!*

Recall the miraculous multiplication of five loaves and two fish which fed, at the very least, 5,000 men, not counting women and children.

The townspeople were so fascinated to hear the words from the Master in an all-day outdoor meeting. The sun was soon to set and the disciples implored Jesus to send the throng away so that they could buy food for themselves in the local stores before closing.

Jesus said, "You feed them!"

Not understanding the wisdom and power of the Lord, the disciples responded, "Oh, you want us to go out and buy it for them and bring it here?" But, after thinking that through, they decided that they didn't even have enough money to pay for the food. None of this seemed to be making any type of sense at all.

But they had forgotten that Jesus could even change water into wine.

Andrew, one of the disciples, pointed to a little boy with five loaves and two fishes: "But what is that among so many?"

Jesus took that morsel of food, gave thanks to the Father, and began to distribute the food among the crowd. The more He gave away, the more was replenished. When they had all eaten to the full, there was so much food leftover that 12 baskets were filled to the brim.

God not only provides, but he provides abundantly.

Remember that when God sets up many communes and places of safety around the world where God's people are protected during the Great Tribulation. There the Lord can supernaturally provide nutrition for His people and nourishment for their souls. [Related scriptures: Mt 14:13-21; Mk 6:30-44; Lk 9:10-17; 2 Kings 4:42-44; Jn 6:1-15; Mt 6:25-26, 31-33; Mk 6:8; Lk 9:3, 10:4, 12:22-23, 22:35].

10 – Hearing God's Voice

You've often heard test drills of the Emergency Broadcast System on radio and TV. Accompanied with a high-pitched tone, the announcer states, "This is a test. For the next 30 seconds this station will conduct a test of the Emergency Broadcast System..."

This national warning system was set up by the U.S. Government to alert the populace of an actual national emergency, be it war, threat of war, natural crisis or disaster.

It was deemed imperative for a line of communication to be opened between the President and the public in the event of an actual emergency.

The Holy Spirit's job is quite similar. He is compelled to help, guide, instruct the saints in all situations, and very often in dire situations. "My sheep hear My voice," says the Lord.

And we're going to find that hearing God's voice from here on end is a definite criteria for navigating the treacherous roads ahead.

Elijah the Prophet serves as a great example. He had just pronounced judgment over Israel for its apostasy, which was orchestrated by Jezebel. Then when he decreed that neither rain nor dew should appear in Israel except at his word, he was just as impacted by the drought as everyone else.

So where could one go during times of national emergencies in ancient Israel? How could they tune in to hear the Ancient Israel Emergency Broadcast System?

Were they godforsaken? God forbid! That's the job of the Holy Spirit! Not one is overlooked, forgotten or misplaced on God's master chessboard.

The Lord spoke to him and said, "Depart from here and settle by the brook Cherith. There you will drink from the brook and I will command ravens to bring you food."

And, sure enough, while there by the brook, the ravens brought Elijah "bread and meat" twice a day.

God doesn't miss a beat. He knows our needs even before we tell Him, and He prepares places for us where we will be nourished. Hence, the importance of hearing the voice of God.

Elijah needed to be in a perpetual state of hearing from the Lord, just like the Israelites of old who also followed the voice of the Lord as they traveled from Egypt to the Promised Land. The Lord showed them exactly where and when to set up camp and when to resume travel again. God always provided them nourishment throughout the journey, even if He had to create food out of nowhere, even in the form of manna!

And, like the pattern set in the Exodus, soon the Lord prompted Elijah to move on.

"Go to Zarephath," said the Lord, "I have commanded a widow to feed you there." God conveniently omitted the fact that the widow was destitute of provisions and near starvation, but that's all within the miracle-working capability of God anyway.

When Elijah arrived, he met the widow and asked her for bread. She knew he was a prophet, but she despondently replied that "as certain as the Lord your God lives" she didn't have anything to give him. She was actually just now preparing her last meal for her son and herself with the last bit of flour and oil that she had. Elijah then calmly said to her, "Prepare for me a small portion first, then provide for yourselves," in a gesture meant to confer a "prophet's reward" upon her (Mt 10:41). Then he prophesied, "Thus says the Lord, neither your bin of flour nor cruise of oil will be used up until rain falls again."

And, so it was, the little she had was sufficiently multiplied over the course of time to sustain her and her son until it rained over the land again.

God heard the cry of this woman and provided a miraculous way for her survival throughout a period of time that resembled, in a manner of speaking, the Great Tribulation. [Related scriptures: 1 Kings 17:1-24; Mt 18:10-14; Ex 16:31].

WHO HAS EARS TO HEAR, LET HIM HEAR

All throughout this chapter, we've been trying to lift up the readers' hopes beyond what their physical senses tell them and to arouse that part of their spirit that says, "Yes, God still performs miracles for His people" and "He loves me enough to perform them just for me!"

Paul assures us that:

Whatsoever things were written aforetime were written for our learning, that we through patience and comfort of the scriptures might have hope (Rom 15:4).

The scriptures have shown us that we should put our trust in our Blessed Hope, Jesus Christ. And it is in Him that we need to find solace, guidance and rescue.

So should you stockpile food for the Tribulation? Should you build an underground shelter? The simple answer is that you should do what the Lord tells you to do!

Don't be afraid. This may be a new concept for many. But Jesus wants us to hear His voice. It's not difficult to hear God. We just need to be aware that He *is* speaking to us.

And it's not true that we have to immerse ourselves into hours of personal worship in order to hear from the Holy Spirit. That may be true if you want to have a heavenly experience, but it's not true if you want to simply hear from the Holy Spirit. It is because of man's difficulty in entering heavenly dimensions that the Lord has seen fit to give us the Holy Spirit to easily enter into our own physical dimension.

The greatest impediment to hearing God is thinking that He doesn't talk with us. But God's word promises that He does talk with us.

- *My sheep hear My voice* (Jn 10:27, NLT throughout)
- *When the Spirit of truth comes, he will guide you into all truth. He will not speak on his own but will tell you what he has heard. He will tell you about the future* (Jn 16:13)
- *And when you are brought to trial in the synagogues and before rulers and authorities, don't worry about how to defend yourself or what to say, for the Holy Spirit will teach you at that time what needs to be said* (Lk 12:11-12)
- *But when the Father sends the Advocate as my representative—that is, the Holy Spirit—he will teach you everything and will remind you of everything I have told you* (Jn 14:26)
- *What I tell you now in the darkness, shout abroad when daybreak comes. What I whisper in your ear, shout from the housetops for all to hear!* (Mt 10:27)

I know this sounds incredible but God desires that we get so close to Him that we get instant answers for immediate concerns.

It is God's will that we allow the Holy Spirit, Who was sent to us after Christ's ascension into heaven, to guide, lead and direct us -- even in our most intimate and vulnerable, personal concerns we have.

You'll notice that Jesus Himself says this very thing. Take a look at the above scripture in Luke 12. He says that when we are called upon to account for certain beliefs we hold the Holy Spirit will speak to us instantly about what to say, in a way that no one can gainsay. That's *instant answers!*

FOUR WAYS OF HEARING GOD'S VOICE

You'll be surprised to know that you've probably already heard God speak to you multiple times. We'll prove that as we examine the four primary ways in which God can speak to His people. The first way is so common that you'll probably have to admit that God has already spoken to you. And once you realize that, you'll be open to the other ways in which God can speak to you.

1 - INNER WITNESS

God speaks primarily through the *Inner Witness* -- that's your *conscience!* How many times has your conscience warned you about not sinning? How many times has your conscience *bothered* you when you were doing something wrong? Guess what? God has been speaking to you!

> *They demonstrate that God's law is written in their hearts, for their own conscience and thoughts either accuse them or tell them they are doing right* (Rom 2:15, NLT).

The *Inner Witness* can also help us to know when we're on the right track. There's a peace that is evident inside of you. But it's important to agree with your conscience so that you're open to the other ways God speaks to us.

But beware. Continually rejecting your conscience hardens you to the point of not being able to hear God anymore (I Tim 4:2).

But rest assured. You do hear from God. From the very first time that your heart was tugging at you to turn to Jesus, you were hearing God. So now that we've proven that God does speak to you, be open to these other ways.

2 - DREAMS & VISIONS
Another very common way the Lord speaks to us is through *Dreams and Visions.* There are many examples in the scriptures that show God speaking to His people through *dreams and visions.* Joseph had a dream, informing him to depart Judea for a time until it was safe for the infant Jesus to return (Mt 2:12). King Nebuchadnezzar had several dreams (Dan 2, 4). In the New Testament, when direction was needed for the early Church, visions were given to both Apostles Paul (Acts 16:9; 18:9) and Peter (Acts 10).

Quite often you need discernment in determining which dreams come from God and which come from pepperoni pizza. But expect God to speak to you in dreams and visions. Recall what God says about the time we're living in presently:

> *And it shall come to pass afterward* [in the last days, Cp Acts 2:17], *that I will pour out my spirit upon all flesh; and your sons and your daughters shall prophesy, your old men shall dream dreams, your young men shall see visions* (Joel 2:28).

Keep a journal for everything you dream or hear from the Lord. Some use notebooks, but I like to type them into a

Word document so that I can easily search for entries later on and carry it around with me on a mobile phone.

So don't take for granted what you see in dreams and visions. God does indeed talk to us this way.

3 – REVELATION

Revelation is another way God speaks to us. *Revelation* is best expressed as *spiritual understanding* that bypasses the natural senses. You don't see it with your eyes, but you see it in your spirit. You don't hear it with your ears, but you hear it in your spirit. It is knowledge and revelation that is deposited within your spirit, in the same way that the Spiritual Gifts expressed in I Corinthians 12 operate: *Gift of Knowledge, Gift of Wisdom, Prophecy, Interpretation, Faith, Discernment.* They are all dropped into your spirit by the Holy Spirit.

They are not necessarily *spoken words* but an *understanding of truth* that is expressed far more powerfully by a small deposit in the spirit than in multiply words in the physical. Similarly, the Lord explained that to me when He told me, *"I will guide you in the way that you should go, directing you to go to the right or left. Listen to My heartbeat. Hearing My heartbeat and moving on it is a far deeper level of intimacy than if you just hear My words."*

Here the Lord directed me to be open to His *heartbeat* – something that can only be understood as *internal* and *non-verbal communication.* God offers that to us too. Therefore, as I Corinthians 12:31 tells us, we need to *earnestly desire* these awesome, wonderful gifts!

4 - INNER VOICE

Then there's the *Inner Voice.* That's the voice that you hear internally in your spirit. At rare times it may be an audible voice, as if someone is in the room with you. But more frequently, it's a *"still, small voice,"* the kind that Elijah heard (I Kings 19:12). It's not flashy or shattering, like wind, fire or earthquake. It's a *"still, small voice,"* the kind that you can overlook or dismiss if you're not intently listening to Him or if you've built a wall of disbelief that prevents you from listening. Philip suddenly heard that voice in his spirit when he was reading the word:

> *Then the Spirit said unto Philip, Go near, and join thyself to this chariot* (Acts 8:29).

This is the *"still, small voice"* you can train yourself to hear.

HOW TO FINE-TUNE HEARING GOD'S VOICE

Despite the fact that mankind has had a difficult time getting up to God's level to hear Him, the Holy Spirit was given to mankind to come down to "our" level, so that we can hear words from the Throne. No striving to get into God's presence, or working ourselves up to hear Him, the Holy Spirit was sent to speak to us on a daily basis, to lead us day by day, in a normal, natural fashion for Christians.

But there are certain things we need to keep in mind in order to have an open and ongoing communication with the Holy Spirit.

Firstly, we are assuming that you've received Jesus as your Savior, repented of your sins and now live for Him. If your heart is towards Him, submitted to Him, and open to receive His directions for your life, then you're on your way to hearing Him.

Secondly, try to regularly maintain a constant recognition that the Holy Spirit is always with you. Communicate consistently with Him. If you're driving alone, you're not alone. Communicate with the Holy Spirit, as if He is driving with you – *for He is!* – all through the day!

Thirdly, as in all normal love relationships, we spend

quality time with our Lover. We get to know our Lover when we spend time with each other. The more we spend time, the more we intensely desire to be in our Lover's presence.

Fourthly, be still before Him. Make it a habit to find a quiet spot to hear from Him. Quite often Jesus went up to a solitary place to worship and to hear from God, or He went into a prayer closet and closed the door. Get the phone and other distractions out of the room, if you have to. Pray to Him with your whole heart, then wait in His presence until you sense an impression from Him. Train yourself to quietly sit before Him. Start with 15 minutes, graduate to an hour or more. The more you do this, the more you'll train yourself to hear from the Master.

IN SUMMARY

We hope this has been an invaluable tool to help you navigate the difficult road ahead until the long awaited return of Jesus Christ.

Perhaps now we'll be able to read much of God's word with more clarity than before. We've been able to highlight certain end-time landmarks in the Word – landmarks that cannot be moved or misapplied.

We've learned about the landmark event that begins the 70th Week of Daniel; the landmark event that begins the Great Tribulation; the landmark event that separates the Great Tribulation from the Day of the Lord; the landmark event that begins the Day of the Lord; and the landmark event that ushers us into God's glorious presence.

With these landmark pieces firmly in place, you can see where other parts of the puzzle belong.

We've learned how to identify the Antichrist. We've seen that God promises protection during the Great Tribulation to the Philadelphia church. It's a new paradigm for the Church that needs to replace the old one.

The pre-trib teaching was actually a way for people to cope with the fear of the future and to dodge the reality of the scriptures.

Remember, there are only going to be two primary characteristics of the last days: Fear and Faith! And, we want you to be filled with Faith.

In summary, the whole purpose of this volume is twofold:

1) To correct the many errors found in the present-day understanding of the events surrounding the return of Christ, including the pre-trib rapture, and to create a more sound paradigm for the church's eschatological blueprint.

2) To inspire the reader to seek the only sure hope during the Great Tribulation – Jesus Christ. Hopefully we draw so close to Him now and fall so much in love with Him now, that, when the time of trouble comes, He will lead us and guide us by the voice of the Holy Spirit and that we find comfort and hope in His Fatherly protection via his angelic hosts.

We bless the reader now with the promise of Christ's words that we may be accounted worthy to escape the Great Tribulation:

Watch ye therefore, and pray always, that ye may be accounted worthy to escape all these things that shall come to pass, and to stand before the Son of man (Lk 21:36).

11
SCRIPTURE COMPENDIUM: PROTECTION DURING TIMES OF TROUBLE

But the previous night God had appeared to Laban the Aramean in a dream and told him, "I'm warning you—leave Jacob alone!" (Gen 31:24, NLT)

Only in the land of Goshen, where the Israelites lived, was there no hail (Ex 9:26, NET)

You yourselves have seen what I did to Egypt and how I lifted you on eagles' wings and brought you to myself (Ex 19:4, NET)

"I am going to send an angel before you to protect you as you journey and to bring you into the place that I have prepared (Ex 23:20, NET)

The LORD your God is about to go ahead of you; he will fight for you, just as you saw him do in Egypt (Deut 1:30, NET)

Of Benjamin he said: The beloved of the LORD will live safely by him; he protects him all the time, and the LORD places him on his chest (Deut 33:12, NET)

He will keep the feet of his saints, and the wicked shall be silent in darkness; for by strength shall no man prevail (1 Sam 2:9, KJV)

In the same way that I valued your life this day, may the LORD value my life and deliver me from all danger (1 Sam 26:24, NET)

The God of my rock; in him will I trust: he is my shield, and the horn of my salvation, my high tower, and my refuge, my saviour; thou savest me from violence. I will call on the LORD, who is worthy to be praised: so shall I be saved from mine enemies (2 Sam 22:3-4, KJV)

You deliver oppressed people, but you watch the proud and bring them down (2 Sam 22:28, NET)

The jar of flour was never empty and the jug of oil never ran out, just as the LORD had promised through Elijah (1 Kings 17:16, NET)

Certainly the LORD watches the whole earth carefully and is ready to strengthen those who are devoted to him... (2 Chr 16:9, NET)

He said: "Pay attention, all you people of Judah, residents of Jerusalem, and King Jehoshaphat! This is what the LORD says to you: 'Don't be afraid and don't panic because of this huge army! For the battle is not yours, but God's'" (2 Chr 20:15, NET)

The LORD is good, indeed, he is a fortress in time of distress, and he protects those who seek refuge in him (Nah 1:7, NET)

Have you not made a hedge around him and his household and all that he has on every side? You have blessed the work of his hands, and his livestock have increased in the land (Job 1:10, NET)

He will deliver you from six calamities; yes, in seven no evil will touch you (Job 5:19, NET)

You will laugh at destruction and famine and need not be afraid of the beasts of the earth (Job 5:22, NET)

And you will be secure, because there is hope; you will be protected and will take your rest in safety. You will lie down with no one to make you afraid, and many will seek your favor (Job 11:18-19, NET)

But you, LORD, are a shield that protects me; you are my glory and the one who restores me (Ps 3:3, NET)

I will lie down and sleep peacefully, for you, LORD, make me safe and secure (Ps 4:8, NET)

But let all who put their trust in You rejoice; let them always shout for joy, because You defend them. And let those who love Your name be joyful in You (Ps 5:11, MKJV)

Consequently the LORD provides safety for the oppressed; he provides safety in times of trouble (Ps 9:9, NET)

You have seen it; for You behold mischief and vexation, to repay it with Your hand. The poor commits himself to You; You are the Helper of the fatherless. Break the arm of the wicked and the evil one; seek out his wickedness, until You find none.

Jehovah is King forever and ever; the nations have perished out of His land. Jehovah, You have heard the desire of the humble; You will prepare their heart, You will cause Your ear to hear, to judge the fatherless and the oppressed, so that the man of the earth may no more terrify (Ps 10:14-18, MKJV)

He rescued me from my strong enemy, from those who hate me, for they were too strong for me (Ps 18:17, NET)

As for God, His way is perfect; the Word of Jehovah is tried; He is a shield to all those who trust in Him (Ps 18:30, MKJV)

For he did not despise or detest the suffering of the oppressed; he did not ignore him; when he cried out to him, he responded (Ps 22:24, NET)

The LORD is my shepherd, I lack nothing. He takes me to lush pastures, he leads me to refreshing water. He restores my strength. He leads me down the right paths for the sake of his reputation. Even when I must walk through the darkest valley, I fear no danger, for you are with me; your rod and your staff reassure me. You prepare a feast before me in plain sight of my enemies. You refresh my head with oil; my cup is completely full. Surely your goodness and faithfulness will pursue me all my days, and I will live in the LORD's house for the rest of my life (Ps 23:1-6, NET)

You shall hide them in the secrecy of Your presence from the pride of man; You shall hide them in a shelter away from the strife of tongues (Ps 31:20, MKJV)

Love the LORD, all you faithful followers of his! The LORD protects those who have integrity, but he pays back in full the one who acts arrogantly (Ps 31:23, NET)

You are my hiding place; You shall preserve me from trouble; You shall circle me with songs of deliverance. Selah (Ps 32:7, MKJV)

The angel of the LORD encamps all around those who fear Him, And delivers them (Ps 34:7, NKJV)

The LORD pays attention to the godly and hears their cry for help (Ps 34:15, NET)

The godly face many dangers, but the LORD saves them from each one of them (Ps 34:19, NET)

How precious is Your loving-kindness, O God! And the sons of men take refuge under the shadow of Your wing (Ps 36:7, MKJV)

Even if he trips, he will not fall headlong, for the LORD holds his hand (Ps 37:24, NET)

But the LORD delivers the godly; he protects them in times of trouble (Ps 37:39, NET)

Blessed is he who considers the poor; The LORD will deliver him in time of trouble. The LORD will preserve him and keep him alive, And he will be blessed on the earth; You will not deliver him to the will of his enemies (Ps 41:1-2, NKJV)

God is our strong refuge; he is truly our helper in times of trouble (Ps 46:1, NET)

Pray to me when you are in trouble! I will deliver you, and you will honor me! (Ps 50:15, NET)

Throw your burden upon the LORD, and he will sustain you.

He will never allow the godly to be upended (Ps 55:22, NET)

Be merciful to me, O God, be merciful to me! For my soul trusts in You; and in the shadow of Your wings I will make my refuge, until these calamities have passed by (Ps 57:1, NKJV)

Indeed, you are my shelter, a strong tower that protects me from the enemy (Ps 61:3, NET)

If only my people would obey me! If only Israel would keep my commands! Then I would quickly subdue their enemies, and attack their adversaries (Ps 81:13-14, NET)

For the LORD God is a sun and shield: the LORD will give grace and glory: no good thing will he withhold from them that walk uprightly. O LORD of hosts, blessed is the man that trusts in thee (Ps 84:11-12, NKJV)

As for you, the one who lives in the shelter of the sovereign One, and resides in the protective shadow of the mighty king —I say this about the LORD, my shelter and my stronghold, my God in whom I trust —he will certainly rescue you from the snare of the hunter and from the destructive plague. He will shelter you with his wings; you will find safety under his wings. His faithfulness is like a shield or a protective wall. You need not fear the terrors of the night, the arrow that flies by day, the plague that comes in the darkness, or the disease that comes at noon. Though a thousand may fall beside you, and a multitude on your right side, it will not reach you. Certainly you will see it with your very own eyes — you will see the wicked paid back. For you have taken refuge in the LORD, my shelter, the sovereign One. No harm will overtake you; no illness will come near your home. For he will order his angels to protect you in all you do. They will lift you up in their hands, so you will not slip and fall on a stone. You will subdue a lion and a snake; you will trample underfoot a young lion and a serpent. The LORD says, "Because he is devoted to me, I will deliver him; I will protect him because he is loyal to me. When he calls out to me, I will answer him. I will be with him when he is in trouble; I will rescue him and bring him honor. I will satisfy him with long life, and will let him see my salvation (Ps 91:1-16, NET)

You who love the LORD, hate evil! He protects the lives of his faithful followers; he delivers them from the power of the wicked (Ps 97:10, NET)

He does not fear bad news. He is confident; he trusts in the LORD (Ps 112:7, NET)

Behold, he that keeps Israel shall neither slumber nor sleep. The LORD is thy keeper: the LORD is thy shade upon thy right hand. The sun shall not smite thee by day, nor the moon by night. The LORD shall preserve thee from all evil: he shall preserve thy soul. The LORD shall preserve thy going out and thy coming in from this time forth, and even for evermore (Ps 121:4-8, NKJV)

Even when I must walk in the midst of danger, you revive me. You oppose my angry enemies, and your right hand delivers me (Ps 138:7, NET)

O LORD, rescue me from wicked men! Protect me from violent men (Ps 140:1, NET)

But the one who listens to me will live in security, and will be at ease from the dread of harm (Pro 1:33, NET)

For wisdom will enter your heart, and moral knowledge will be attractive to you. Discretion will protect you, understanding will guard you, to deliver you from the way of the wicked, from those speaking perversity, who leave the upright paths to walk on the dark ways (Pro 2:10-13, NET)

Acknowledge him in all your ways, and he will make your paths straight (Pro 3:6, NET)

My son, do not let them (His words) depart from your eyes; keep sound wisdom and judgment, and they shall be life to your soul and grace to your neck; then you shall walk in your way safely, and your foot shall not stumble. When you lie down, you shall not be afraid; yea, you shall lie down, and your sleep shall be sweet (Pro 3:21-24, MKJV)

The LORD satisfies the appetite of the righteous, but he thwarts the craving of the wicked (Pro 10:3, NET)

The righteous person is delivered out of trouble, and the wicked turns up in his stead (Pro 11:8, NET)

In the fear of the LORD one has strong confidence, and it will be a refuge for his children (Pro 14:26, NET)

The name of the LORD is a strong tower: the righteous runs into it, and is safe (Pro 18:10, NKJV)

The fear of man brings a snare, but whoever trusts in the Lord shall be safe (Pro 29:25, NKJV)

Every word of God is pure: he is a shield unto them that put their trust in him (Pro 30:5, NKJV)

You will hear a word spoken behind you, saying, "This is the correct way, walk in it," whether you are heading to the right or the left (Isa 30:21, NET)

This is the person who will live in a secure place; he will find safety in the rocky, mountain strongholds; he will have food and a constant supply of water. You will see a king in his splendor; you will see a wide land (Isa 33:16-17, NET)

Don't be afraid, for I am with you! Don't be frightened, for I am your God! I strengthen you — yes, I help you — yes, I uphold you with my saving right hand! (Isa 41:10, NET)

Now, this is what the LORD says, the one who created you, O Jacob, and formed you, O Israel: "Don't be afraid, for I will protect you. I call you by name, you are mine. When you pass through the waters, I am with you; when you pass through the streams, they will not overwhelm you. When you walk through the fire, you will not be burned; the flames will not harm you" (Isa 43:1-2, NET)

"You will be reestablished when I vindicate you. You will not experience oppression; indeed, you will not be afraid. You will not be terrified, for nothing frightening will come near you. If anyone dares to challenge you, it will not be my doing! Whoever tries to challenge you will be defeated. Look, I create the craftsman, who fans the coals into a fire and forges a weapon. I create the destroyer so he might devastate. No weapon forged to be used against you will succeed; you will refute everyone who tries to accuse you. This is what the LORD will do for his servants — I will vindicate them," says the LORD (Isa 54:14-17, NET)

The LORD will continually lead you; he will feed you even in parched regions. He will give you renewed strength, and you will be like a well-watered garden, like a spring that continually produces water (Isa 58:11, NET)

They will attack you but they will not be able to overcome you, for I will be with you to rescue you, says the LORD (Jer

1:19, NET)

For this is what the sovereign LORD says: Look, I myself will search for my sheep and seek them out (Ezek 34:11, NET)

Nebuchadnezzar spoke, saying, Blessed be the God of Shadrach, Meshach, and Abednego, who sent His Angel and delivered His servants who trusted in Him, and they have frustrated the king's word, and yielded their bodies, that they should not serve nor worship any god except their own God! (Dan 3:28, NKJV)

Then Daniel said to the king, "O king, live forever! "My God sent His angel and shut the lions' mouths, so that they have not hurt me, because I was found innocent before Him; and also, O king, I have done no wrong before you" (Dan 6:21-22, NKJV)

Then with smooth words he will defile those who have rejected the covenant. But the people who are loyal to their God will act valiantly (Dan 11:32, NET)

*At that time Michael, the great prince who watches over your people, will arise. There will be a time of distress unlike any other from the nation's beginning up to that time. But at that time your own people, all those whose names are found written in the book, will escape (*Dan 12:1, NET)

For I, saith the LORD, will be unto her a wall of fire round about, and will be the glory in the midst of her (Zech 2:5, KJV)

And do not lead us into temptation (trials), but deliver us from the evil one (Mt 6:13, NET)

Whenever they hand you over for trial, do not worry about how to speak or what to say, for what you should say will be given to you at that time (Mt 10:19, NET)

Do not be afraid of those who kill the body but cannot kill the soul. Instead, fear the one who is able to destroy both soul and body in hell. Aren't two sparrows sold for a penny? Yet not one of them falls to the ground apart from your Father's will. Even all the hairs on your head are numbered. So do not be afraid; you are more valuable than many sparrows (Mt 10:28-31, NET)

Take heed that you do not despise one of these little ones, for I say to you that in heaven their angels always see the face of My Father who is in heaven (Mt 18:10, NKJV)

And if those days had not been cut short, no one would be saved. But for the sake of the elect those days will be cut short (Mt 24:22, NET)

Look, I have given you authority to tread on snakes and scorpions and on the full force of the enemy, and nothing will hurt you (Lk 10:19, NET)

Won't God give justice to his chosen ones, who cry out to him day and night? Will he delay long to help them? I tell you, he will give them justice speedily. Nevertheless, when the Son of Man comes, will he find faith on earth?" (Lk 18:7-8, NET)

Yet not a hair of your head will perish (Lk 21:18, NET)

But stay alert at all times, praying that you may have strength to escape all these things that must happen, and to stand before the Son of Man (Lk 21:36, NET)

Then Jesus said to them, "When I sent you out with no money bag, or traveler's bag, or sandals, you didn't lack anything, did you?" They replied, "Nothing." (Lk 22:35, NET)

Our ancestors ate the manna in the wilderness, just as it is written, 'He gave them bread from heaven to eat' (Jn 6:31, NET)

I will not leave you orphans. I will come to you (Jn 14:18, MKJV)

Peace I leave with you, My peace I give to you. Not as the world gives do I give to you. Let not your heart be troubled, neither let it be afraid (Jn 14:27, MKJV)

I have spoken these things to you so that you might have peace in Me. In the world you shall have tribulation, but be of good cheer. I have overcome the world (Jn 16:33, MKJV)

And now I am in the world no longer, but these are in the world, and I come to You, Holy Father. Keep them in Your name, those whom You have given Me, so that they may be one as We are. While I was with them in the world, I kept them in Your name. Those that You have given Me I have kept, and none of them is lost, but the son of perdition, that the scripture might be fulfilled. And now I come to You, and these things I speak in the world that they might have My joy fulfilled in them. I have given them Your Word, and the world has hated them because they are not of the world, even as I am not of the world. I do not pray for You to take them out of the world, but for You to keep them from the evil. They are not of the world, even as I am not of the world. Sanctify them through Your truth. Your Word is truth. As You have sent Me into the world, even so I have sent them into the world. And I sanctify Myself for their sakes, so that they also might be sanctified in truth (Jn 17:11-19, MKJV)

What then shall we say about these things? If God is for us, who can be against us? (Rom 8:31, NET)

Who shall separate us from the love of Christ? Shall tribulation, or distress, or persecution, or famine, or nakedness, or peril, or sword? As it is written, "For Your sake we are killed all the day long. We are counted as sheep of slaughter." But in all these things we more than conquer through Him who loved us. For I am persuaded that neither death, nor life, nor angels, nor principalities, nor powers, nor things present, nor things to come, nor height, nor depth, nor any other creature, shall be able to separate us from the love of God which is in Christ Jesus our Lord (Rom 8:35-39, MKJV)

For everything that was written in former times was written for our instruction, so that through endurance and through encouragement of the scriptures we may have hope (Rom 15:4, NET)

These things happened to them as examples and were written for our instruction, on whom the ends of the ages have come (1 Cor 10:11, NET)

No trial has overtaken you that is not faced by others. And God is faithful: He will not let you be tried beyond what you are able to bear, but with the trial will also provide a way out so that you may be able to endure it (1 Cor 10:13, NET)

(Love) always protects, always trusts, always hopes, always perseveres (1 Cor 13:7, NIV)

But he said to me, "My grace is enough for you, for my power is made perfect in weakness." So then, I will boast most gladly about my weaknesses, so that the power of Christ may reside in me (2 Cor 12:9, NET)

For this reason, take up the full armor of God so that you may be able to stand your ground on the evil day, and having done everything, to stand (Eph 6:13, NET)

And I am convinced and sure of this very thing, that He Who began a good work in you will continue until the day of Jesus Christ [right up to the time of His return], *developing* [that good work] *and perfecting and bringing it to full completion in you* (Phil 1:6, Amplified)

He has delivered us from the power of darkness and conveyed us into the kingdom of the Son of His love (Col 1:13, NKJV)

For we tell you this by the word of the Lord, that we who are alive, who are left until the coming of the Lord, will surely not go ahead of those who have fallen asleep. For the Lord himself will come down from heaven with a shout of command, with the voice of the archangel, and with the trumpet of God, and the dead in Christ will rise first. Then we who are alive, who are left, will be suddenly caught up together with them in the clouds to meet the Lord in the air. And so we will always be with the Lord. Therefore encourage one another with these words (1 Thess 4:15-18, NET)

But the Lord is faithful, and he will strengthen you and protect you from the evil one (2 Thess 3:3, NET)

For God has not given us the spirit of fear, but of power and of love and of a sound mind (2 Tim 1:7, MKJV)

...as well as the persecutions and sufferings that happened to me in Antioch, in Iconium, and in Lystra. I endured these persecutions and the Lord delivered me from them all. Now in fact all who want to live godly lives in Christ Jesus will be persecuted (2 Tim 3:11-12, NET)

Are they not all ministering spirits, sent out to serve those who will inherit salvation? (Heb 1:14, NET)

... for He has said, "Not at all will I leave you, not at all will I forsake you, never!" so that we may boldly say, "The Lord is my helper, and I will not fear what man shall do to me" (Heb 13:5-6, MKJV)

For the eyes of the Lord are upon the righteous and his ears are open to their prayer. But the Lord's face is against those who do evil. For who is going to harm you if you are devoted to what is good? (1 Pet 3:12-13, NET)

And He did not spare the old world, but saved Noah the eighth one, a preacher of righteousness, bringing in the flood upon the world of the ungodly. And turning the cities of Sodom and Gomorrah into ashes, He condemned them with an overthrow, setting an example to men intending to live ungodly. And He delivered righteous Lot, oppressed with the lustful behavior of the lawless. For that righteous one living among them, in seeing and hearing, his righteous soul was tormented from day to day with their unlawful deeds. The Lord knows how to deliver the godly out of temptation, and to reserve the unjust for a day of judgment, to be punished (2 Pet 2:5-9, MKJV)

You are from God, little children, and have conquered them, because the one who is in you is greater than the one who is in the world (1 Jn 4:4, NET)

Because you have kept my admonition to endure steadfastly, I will also keep you from the hour of testing that is about to come on the whole world to test those who live on the earth (Rev 3:10, NET)

... and she fled into the wilderness where a place had been prepared for her by God, so she could be taken care of for 1,260 days (Rev 12:6, NET)

But the woman was given the two wings of a giant eagle so that she could fly out into the wilderness, to the place God prepared for her, where she is taken care of — away from the presence of the serpent — for a time, times, and half a time. Then the serpent spouted water like a river out of his mouth after the woman in an attempt to sweep her away by a flood, but the earth came to her rescue; the ground opened up and swallowed the river that the dragon had spewed from his mouth (Rev 12:14-16, NET)

ABOUT THE AUTHOR

Lou Comunale began his career as a news analyst working in the news departments of well-known news outlets, among them NBC, MSNBC, ABC, and CBS. In his private life, he was also an analyst of biblical prophecy; when the call of God prompted him to combine the two, the foundation was laid for the volume you now hold in your hands.

For nine years, he produced the TV program, "Power for Life with Matt Sorger." Once that work was over, the Lord prompted Lou to write this book because of the urgency of the hour and the need to correct end-time doctrinal error.

Presently, Lou is editor of the News2morrow.com website as well as a producer of the Mindshift teaching videos, the most popular episode being, "John Paul Jackson Prophecy on President Donald Trump." In that episode, produced in January 2016, the Lord showed Lou that Trump was going to be president and then use him as a "Bulldozer" against the plans of man. Furthermore, God was not through with America and that a time of Awakening is now planned.

Lou has appeared on many radio and internet programs, bringing his fresh perspective on biblical prophecy. Speaking engagements (and bulk rates for the book) can be arranged by contacting Lou Comunale at mediamantle@gmail.com.

Follow Lou Comunale on his website & social media:

https://www.news2morrow.com/
https://www.facebook.com/lou.comunale
https://www.facebook.com/LouComunaleAuthor/
https://www.facebook.com/groups/news2morrow/
https://www.youtube.com/user/MediaMantle3
https://twitter.com/LouComunale

Made in the USA
Middletown, DE
18 February 2020